ST

Cookery

Vegetarian

Recipes from Around the World

Sue Townsend and Caroline Young

641.5

4/05

0042894719

www.heinemann.co.uk/library
Visit our website to find out more information about **Heinemann Library** books.

To order:
 Phone 44 (0) 1865 888066
 Send a fax to 44 (0) 1865 314091
Visit the Heinemann Bookshop at www.heinemann.co.uk/library to browse our catalogue and order online.

First published in Great Britain by Heinemann Library, Halley Court, Jordan Hill, Oxford OX2 8EJ, part of Harcourt Education.

Heinemann is a registered trademark of Harcourt Education Ltd.

Editorial: Nancy Dickmann, Andrew Solway and Jennifer Tubbs
Design: Jo Hinton-Malivoire and Tinstar Design Limited (www.tinstar.co.uk)
Illustrations: Nicholas Beresford-Davies
Picture Research: Catherine Bevan
Production: Séverine Ribierre

Originated by Dot Gradations Ltd
Printed in China
by WKT Company Limited

ISBN 0 431 11730 6 (hardback)
07 06 05 04 03
10 9 8 7 6 5 4 3 2 1

ISBN 0 431 11737 3 (paperback)
08 07 06 05 04
10 9 8 7 6 5 4 3 2 1

British Library Cataloguing in Publication Data
Townsend, Sue & Young, Caroline
Vegetarian. – (A World of Recipes)
641.5'123
A full catalogue record for this book is available from the British Library.

Acknowledgements
The publishers would like to thank the following for permission to reproduce photographs: Corbis: p. 6; Gareth Boden: all other photographs.

Cover photographs reproduced with permission of Gareth Boden.

Every effort has been made to contact copyright holders of any material reproduced in this book. Any omissions will be rectified in subsequent printings if notice is given to the publishers.

Contents

Key

* easy

** medium

*** difficult

Words appearing in the text in bold, **like this**, are explained in the glossary.

Vegetarian food

Many people in the world are **vegetarian**. This means that they do not eat any meat. Some vegetarians eat fish, but no meat. Other vegetarians, called **vegans**, do not eat any food that has come from an animal, including milk and eggs. Instead of dairy products, they may eat foods made with soya milk, from soya beans. Whatever people eat, it is important to make sure that their body is getting the **nutrients** it needs.

Is it healthy to be a vegetarian?

Animal foods, such as meat, fish and eggs, contain **protein**, which our bodies need to stay healthy. Fruit, **pulses** and vegetables do not have as much protein as animal foods, but eating a good range of them will give you all the protein you need. Here are some examples:

squash

cabbage

pineapple

swede

peas

lemon

red peppers

potatoes

sweetcorn

yoghurt

carrots

apples

onion

turnips

garlic

ginger

pecans

bread

cheese

beans

leeks

cinnamon

Pulses

Pulses are beans and seeds from plants. They include broad beans, black-eyed beans and chick peas. Pulses are a very good source of protein and can be cooked in many different ways. You can buy most pulses dried or tinned.

Nuts

Nuts, such as walnuts, pecan nuts and peanuts, are another good source of protein. Many cooking styles around the world use nuts in sweet and savoury recipes. Nuts contain quite a lot of fat, so do not eat too many.

Dairy or soya products

Milk, cheese and yoghurt are dairy products. They contain protein and **calcium**, which help to give us strong bones and teeth. Vegans can get calcium from dairy substitutes, such as soya milk with added calcium. Supermarkets sell both types of products.

Fruit and vegetables

Fruit and vegetables are a good source of **vitamins**, which everyone needs to stay healthy. You can buy many different kinds of fruit and vegetables in supermarkets and grocery shops. They come from all over the world. Dried fruit, and canned and frozen fruit and vegetables, contain nutrients, too.

Cereals

More people in the world eat rice every day than any other food. It is a **staple** ingredient in many countries. People also eat other cereals, such as wheat and barley. Health food shops sell a variety of grains, including bulgur wheat.

Around the world

There are more **vegetarians** today than there have ever been, and their numbers are growing. There are several reasons why people choose not to eat meat.

Why are people vegetarian?

In poorer parts of the world, people may have no choice about being vegetarian. Meat is a luxury food that they cannot afford. Some families keep a cow, goat or chicken for their milk or their eggs, but their animal is too valuable to kill for meat.

Many millions of people avoid eating meat for religious reasons. The followers of Hinduism and Buddhism, for example, believe that they should respect all living beings and live in a way that does not cause any harm. Because of this, many are vegetarians.

▶ *A wide variety of vegetables are being sold at this market stall in India.*

Other vegetarians have made a choice not to eat meat. They believe that it is wrong to breed and kill other living things for our food. Many people feel that they will enjoy better health if they follow a vegetarian diet, so they do not eat meat.

The vegetarian world

There are vegetarians in every part of the world. The recipes in this book come from all around the world. The map below shows you where the countries which the recipes come from, are located.

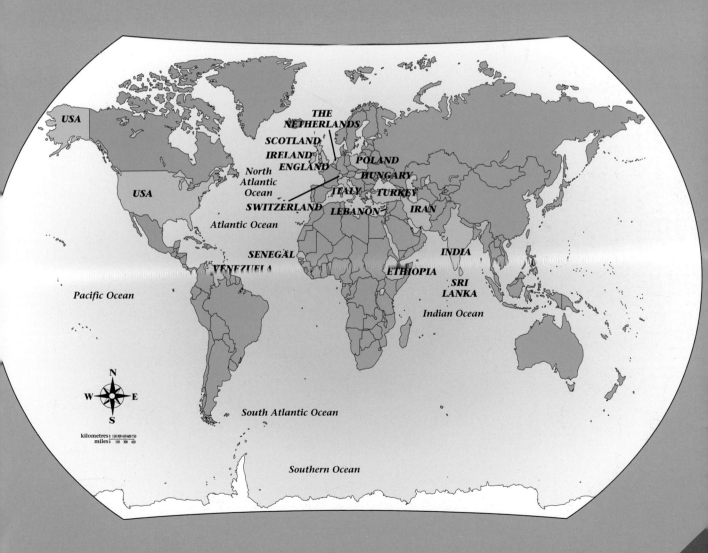

Before you start

Kitchen rules

There are a few basic rules you should always follow when you are cooking:

- Ask an adult if you can use the kitchen.
- Some cooking processes, especially those involving hot water or oil, can be dangerous. When you see this sign, take extra care or ask an adult to help.
- Wash your hands before you start.
- Wear an apron to protect your clothes.
- Be very careful when you use sharp knives.
- Never leave pan handles sticking out, in case you knock them.
- Always use oven gloves to lift things in and out of the oven.
- Wash fruit and vegetables before you use them.
- Always wash chopping boards very well after use, especially after chopping raw meat, fish or poultry.
- Use a separate chopping board for onions and garlic, if possible.

How long will it take?

Some of these recipes are quick and easy, and some are more difficult and take longer. The strip across the right-hand side of each recipe page tells you how long it takes to prepare a dish from start to finish. It also shows how difficult it is to make: each recipe is * (easy), ** (medium) or *** (difficult).

Quantities and measurements

You can see how many people each recipe will serve at the top of each right-hand page. You can multiply or divide the quantities if you want to cook for more or fewer people.

Ingredients for recipes can be measured in two different ways. Metric measurements use grams and millilitres. Imperial measurements use ounces and fluid ounces. This book uses metric measurements. If you want to convert these into imperial measurements, see the chart on page 44.

In the recipes, you will see the following abbreviations:

tbsp = tablespoon   g = grams   cm = centimetres
tsp = teaspoon   ml = millilitres

Utensils

To cook the recipes in this book, you will need these utensils (as well as essentials, such as spoons, plates and bowls):

- plastic or glass chopping board (easier to clean than wooden ones)
- food processor or blender
- large frying pan
- 20 cm heavy-based non-stick frying pan
- measuring jug
- sieve
- small and large saucepans, with lids
- set of scales
- sharp knife
- slotted spoon
- kitchen spatula
- baking sheets
- lemon squeezer
- potato masher
- apple corer
- whisk
- 18 cm plate
- pastry brush.

 Whenever you use kitchen knives, be very careful.

Broad bean pâté with ciabatta toast (Italy)

There are many **vegetarian** recipes from Italy. This one is from Tuscany, an area famous both for its old towns and cities, and for its beautiful countryside. This recipe uses frozen broad beans, because fresh ones are only available for a short time each year. Ciabatta (pronounced *chee-a-batta*) is a type of Italian bread, which you can find in many supermarkets or bakeries. Serve the pâté with some salad as an ideal starter, light lunch or snack.

What you need

1 onion
3 garlic cloves
2 tbsp olive oil
400 g frozen broad beans
70 g reduced-fat
   cream cheese
1 lemon
1 ciabatta loaf

What you do

1 **Peel** and finely **chop** the onion and garlic.

(!) 2 Heat the oil in a small frying pan over a medium heat. **Fry** the onion and garlic for 5 minutes, until they are softened. Leave them to cool.

(!) 3 Put the frozen broad beans into a saucepan and cover them with water. Bring the water to the **boil**, **cover** the pan and **simmer** the beans for 5 minutes.

4 **Drain** the beans and let them cool down.

5 Put them into a food processor or blender. Add the cream cheese and the fried onion mixture.

6 Cut the lemon in half. Using a lemon squeezer, squeeze the juice from both halves.

7 Add the lemon juice to the bean mixture, and **blend** until smooth.

8 Using a spatula, scrape the pâté into a bowl for serving.

9 Cut the ciabatta into 2 cm thick slices. Heat a grill and **toast** the slices of bread on each side, until lightly browned.

10 Serve the ciabatta warm with the pâté and some salad.

Walnut, fenugreek and yoghurt soup (Iran)

For hundreds of years, Iran was in the middle of trading routes between Europe and Asia. Iran's cooking style has been influenced by the many different people who have visited the country throughout history. In Iran, this soup is served hot or cold, as a starter or light lunch. It contains the **ground** seeds of a plant called fenugreek. Fenugreek leaves can be added to salads, too.

What you need

1 onion
1 tbsp vegetable oil
  or butter
50 g walnuts
1 tsp ground
  fenugreek
600 ml water
1 tbsp cornflour
500 ml natural
  yoghurt

What you do

1 **Peel** and finely **chop** the onion.

2 Heat the oil or butter in a saucepan over a medium heat. Add the onion and **fry** over a medium to low heat for 4–5 minutes, until it has softened.

3 Put the walnuts into a blender, and **blend** until finely chopped. Add the walnuts and fenugreek to the saucepan.

4 In a bowl, stir 4 tbsp of the water into the cornflour.

5 Add the rest of the water to the pan. **Cover** and **simmer** for 20 minutes, and then allow to cool for 5 minutes.

⊘ **6** Stir the yoghurt into the cornflour mixture. Add 240 ml of the liquid from the saucepan to the yoghurt mixture, and stir well.

7 Slowly pour the yoghurt mixture into the pan, stirring all the time. Reheat the soup, but do not let it **boil.** Serve hot or cold with some bread.

MAKING YOGHURT

To make your own yoghurt, heat 500 ml of milk until it is just boiling. Let it cool until it is warm, then stir in 2 tbsp plain natural yoghurt. Pour into a clean jar and keep in a warm place for 6–8 hours, until set. **Chill** the yoghurt for 12 hours before serving.

Black-eyed bean cakes (Ethiopia)

Farmers in north and central African countries, such as Ethiopia, grow black-eyed beans, or black-eyed peas, as they are sometimes called. African cooks usually soak the beans, pour them into a bowl and **mash** them with a simple stone or wooden tool. They **deep-fry** their bean cakes, but this version fries them in a little oil.

What you need

200 g dried black-
 eyed beans
150 g sweet potato
1 onion
pinch of salt
half a red chilli (if
 you like them)
1 tbsp flour
3 tbsp oil

What you do

1 Put the black-eyed beans into a bowl, and cover them with cold water. Leave them to soak overnight.

2 **Drain** the beans. Rub them between your hands so that the skins loosen. Put them into a bowl and cover them with water. Tip the water and skins away.

3 **Peel** the sweet potato and cut it into 2 cm chunks. Peel and finely **chop** the onion.

4 Put the potato into a saucepan, cover it with **boiling** water and add a pinch of salt. Cook for 15 minutes, or until it is tender, and then drain it.

5 Cut the half a chilli in half lengthways and throw away the seeds. Chop the chilli finely. Wash your hands thoroughly after handling chilli. The juice can make your eyes and skin very sore.

6 Put the beans into a blender. Add the onion and chilli, and **blend** until smooth. Add the potato and blend again.

7 Sprinkle a little of the flour on to a work surface. Take out 2 tbsp of the mixture, and shape it into a ball. Then flatten it into a fritter shape. Do this with the rest of the mixture, to make about 20 fritters.

(!) 8 Heat the oil in a large frying pan over a medium heat. **Fry** the bean cakes, four or five at a time, for 4 minutes on each side, until golden. Lift the cooked bean cakes on to kitchen paper.

9 Serve straightaway, with cooked, green vegetables or salad, as a starter or light lunch.

Gobi paratha (India)

Many people in India are **vegetarian**. They cook different dishes using vegetables and **pulses**. In India, people often scoop up their food with flat breads, such as parathas. This recipe is for a paratha stuffed with vegetables. Parathas can also be flavoured with spices or fried onion.

What you need

100 g cauliflower florets
1 tsp salt
1 onion
quarter of a green chilli
    (if you like them)
2.5 cm piece fresh ginger
1 tbsp fresh coriander
    (chopped)
300 g wholewheat flour
4 tbsp ghee (clarified
    butter)
    or vegetable oil

What you do

1 **Chop** or **grate** the cauliflower florets finely, into very small pieces. Tip them into a sieve over the sink. Sprinkle them with some salt, and leave to **drain** for 30 minutes.

2 Meanwhile, **peel** and finely chop the onion.

3 Cut the piece of chilli in half, and throw away the seeds. Chop the chilli finely. Wash your hands thoroughly after touching raw chilli.

4 Peel and grate the ginger. Rinse the cauliflower pieces and pat them dry.

5 Put the cauliflower, onion, chilli, ginger and coriander into a bowl, and stir well.

6 Put the flour into a bowl, add 2 tbsp ghee or vegetable oil, and a pinch of salt. Stir in 200 ml water. Using your hands, make the mixture into a stiff dough.

7 Sprinkle a little flour on a work surface. Stretch the dough, fold it over, then press it with the palm of your hand. Turn in round by one quarter, and repeat. **Knead** it in this way for 3 minutes.

8 Cut the dough into four pieces. Using a rolling pin, roll each one out to form a 15 cm circle. Brush a little ghee or oil over each.

9 Scatter the cauliflower mixture over the circles. Gather each circle up to make a ball. Carefully roll each ball out into a 22 cm circle.

(!) 10 Brush each paratha with a little ghee or oil. Heat a heavy-based frying pan over a medium heat. **Fry** each paratha for 3–4 minutes on each side, until golden brown.

11 Serve warm with a vegetable curry (see page 36), **chutney** and rice.

Barley and vegetable soup (Poland)

Winters in Poland can be extremely cold, so warm, filling soups such as this one are a popular lunch or supper dish. Polish farmers grow the vegetables this soup contains, as well as many different kinds of fruit. They bottle fruit or make it into jam, before **exporting** it to other countries.

What you need

75 g pearl barley
1.5 litres hot water
1 carrot
1 parsnip
2 potatoes
1 celery stick
2 onions
2 tbsp vegetable oil
50 g button mushrooms
2 vegetable stock cubes
salt and pepper

What you do

1 Put the pearl barley into a bowl and cover it with cold water. Leave it to soak for 4 hours.

(!) 2 **Drain** the barley. Put it into a pan, add half the hot water and bring it to the **boil**. **Cover** the pan and **simmer** for 30 minutes.

3 **Peel** the carrot and parsnip, and trim off both ends. Peel the potatoes.

4 Cut all three vegetables into 1 cm slices, and then into cubes.

5 Trim the ends off the celery. Cut it into 1 cm slices.

6 Peel and **chop** the onions.

(!) 7 Heat the oil in a large saucepan over a medium heat. **Fry** the onion for 3 minutes, or it is until softened. Add the celery, potato, carrot and parsnip. Stir well and cook for 5 minutes, stirring occasionally.

8 **Slice** the mushrooms thinly and add them to the pan.

(!) 9 Add the pearl barley and the liquid it cooked in. Pour in the rest of the hot water.

10 Crumble the stock cubes into the pan, stirring well. Bring to the boil, **cover** and simmer for 20 minutes.

11 Add a pinch of salt and pepper. Spoon the soup into bowls. Serve with crusty bread.

Chick peas with sugar snap peas (Senegal)

Many traditional African dishes are made in one pot, hung over a fire. All the ingredients are cooked together as a complete meal, as in this recipe from Senegal, in north-west Africa. Sugar snap peas are grown throughout Africa.

What you need

1 onion
1 garlic clove
450 g sugar snap peas
2 tomatoes
1 tbsp vegetable oil
1 tsp black mustard seeds
1 tsp **ground** cumin
400 g can chick peas

What you do

1 **Peel** and finely **chop** the onion and garlic.

2 Cut the ends off the sugar snap peas and cut them in half.

3 Chop the tomatoes.

4 Heat the oil in a medium saucepan over a medium heat. Add the onion and garlic, and **fry** for 3 minutes, or until they are softened.

5 Stir in the sugar snap peas and tomatoes and cook for 5 minutes.

6 Add the mustard seeds and cumin, and cook for 1 minute.

7 Empty the chick peas into a sieve. Rinse them under running cold water.

8 Stir the chick peas into the sugar snap peas mixture. **Cover** the pan and cook for 4–5 minutes, until piping hot.

9 Spoon on to a serving dish. Serve straight away.

Colcannon (Ireland)

For centuries, potatoes were a **staple** food in Ireland. If the potato harvest failed, many people starved. Colcannon is a traditional dish that mixes potatoes with spring onions and cabbage. If it is served at Halloween, a silver coin or charm is sometimes stirred into the mixture – whoever gets the charm is supposed to marry within a year.

What you need

750 g potatoes
pinch of salt
half a bunch of
   spring onions
100 g cabbage
100 ml milk
50 g butter

What you do

1 **Peel** the potatoes and cut them into 4 cm chunks. Put them into a pan with a pinch of salt.

2 Cover the potatoes with **boiling** water. Bring the water back to the boil, **cover** and **simmer** for 17 minutes (you may need to set a timer for this).

3 Trim the ends off the spring onions and throw them away. Cut the spring onions into thin **slices**.

4 Wash the cabbage and **chop** it into small pieces.

5 Add the onions and the cabbage to the potatoes in the pan, and cook for a further 3 minutes.

6 Carefully **drain** the potatoes, onions and cabbage into a colander, and then put them back into the hot pan.

7 **Mash** the vegetables with a potato masher. Add enough milk to make a light, fluffy mixture.

8 Stir in half the butter, and some salt and pepper.

9 Put the Colcannon into a serving dish. Make several dips in the top with a teaspoon and put a little bit of the rest of the butter into each dip. Serve hot, with other vegetables.

23

Olive, pomegranate and walnut salad (Turkey)

Summers are very hot in Turkey, so people there usually eat a light lunch. They eat their main meal in the evening, when it is cooler. This recipe is from south-eastern Turkey, where farmers grow all the ingredients – olives, walnuts and pomegranates.

What you need

1 pomegranate
50 g fresh coriander
1 bunch spring onions
120 g walnuts
25 g fresh sorrel or
　spinach leaves
120 g Queen green
　olives

*For the **dressing:***
3 tbsp olive oil
1½ tbsp lemon juice
salt and pepper

What you do

1 Cut the pomegranate in half. Hold each half skin-side up over a bowl, and tap it with a rolling pin so that the seeds drop into the bowl.

2 **Chop** the coriander finely.

3 Trim the ends off the spring onions and throw them away. Cut the spring onions into thin **slices**.

4 Put the walnuts into a blender and **blend** until roughly chopped.

5 Rinse the sorrel or spinach leaves under running cold water, and pat them dry with a clean tea towel. Cut off the tough stalks.

6 Put all the dressing ingredients into a small screw-topped jar.

7 Shake all the salad ingredients together in a bowl. Shake the dressing well, pour it over the salad and toss again.

8 Spoon the salad on to individual plates, and serve with crusty bread.

OLIVES

Olives grow on trees in groups called groves. Some olive trees can produce olives for up to 300 years. The olives are harvested and soaked in salt water for eating, or crushed to make olive oil.

Sweetcorn, pepper and pumpkin stew (Venezuela)

Cooking all the ingredients for a meal in the same pot is part of traditional cooking in Venezuela, South America. Serve this vegetable stew as a main meal with crusty bread or rice.

What you need

2 onions
1 garlic clove
400 g pumpkin or
    butternut squash
2 corns on the cob,
 thawed if frozen
4 tomatoes
1 red pepper
4 small–medium potatoes
2 tbsp vegetable oil
100 g peas, fresh or frozen
1 tbsp fresh
    chopped marjoram

What you do

1 **Peel** and finely **chop** the onions and garlic.

2 Peel the pumpkin or butternut squash, throw away the seeds and cut the flesh into 2 cm chunks.

3 If using fresh corns on the cob, pull the leaves and silky threads off.

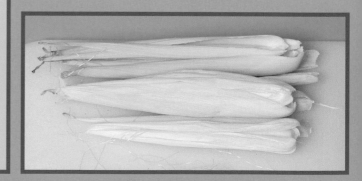

4 Cut the tomatoes into quarters. Cut the pepper in half, and throw away the stalk and seeds. Cut the flesh into 3 cm pieces.

5 Peel the potatoes and cut them into 2 cm chunks.

(!) 6 Heat the oil in a flameproof casserole dish or large pan over a medium heat. **Fry** the onion for 3 minutes, add the garlic and fry for 1 minute more.

7 Add the rest of the prepared vegetables, marjoram, salt and pepper and 450 ml of water to the pan. **Cover** and **simmer** for 25–30 minutes.

8 Using a slotted spoon, lift the sweetcorn on to a board. When it is cool, cut it into 1 cm thick slices.

9 Add the sweetcorn and peas to the pan, and cook for 5 minutes.

10 Stir the stew, and spoon it into a serving dish (if you cooked it in a pan). Serve hot.

Tabbouleh (Lebanon)

Lebanon is in the Middle East, between Israel and Syria. Tabbouleh is a traditional Lebanese recipe, but people all over the Middle East make it. They may change some of the ingredients, depending on what is available locally, but it always includes bulgur wheat. Serve it with **pitta bread** or with other dishes, as a side salad.

What you need

175 g bulgur (or cracked) wheat
1 lemon
2 tbsp olive oil
quarter of a cucumber
2 spring onions
6 cherry tomatoes
4 tbsp chopped fresh parsley
2 tbsp chopped fresh mint

What you do

1 Put the bulgur wheat into a heatproof bowl. Pick out any small stones.

(!) 2 Pour 550 ml **boiling** water over the wheat and stir well. Leave it for 30 minutes, stirring from time to time.

3 Put a sieve over the sink and **drain** the wheat.

4 Cut the lemon in half. Using a lemon squeezer, squeeze the juice from both halves.

5 Stir the lemon juice and olive oil into the bulgur wheat.

6 Cut the cucumber into long slices 1 cm thick, then cut each slice into strips 1 cm thick. Cut across each strip to make 1 cm cubes.

7 Trim the ends off the spring onions. Cut the spring onions into ½ cm slices.

8 Cut the cherry tomatoes in half. Stir the chopped herbs and tomatoes into the bulgur wheat with the cucumber. Add some salt and pepper.

9 Serve straightaway, with pitta bread or crusty bread, or keep it in the fridge (it will keep for up to 2 days).

Winter vegetable goulash (Hungary)

In Hungary, winters are very cold and few things grow. Hungarians store vegetables in a dry, dark place, and cook them with tomatoes and a mild, red spice, paprika, to make this stew, called goulash. Goulash can also have beans or meat as its main ingredient. Serve it as a main dish, with rice, pasta or crusty bread.

What you need

2 onions
2 carrots
2 parsnips
200 g swede
100 g turnip
   (if you like it)
2 tbsp vegetable oil
1 tbsp paprika
2 tbsp plain flour
8 small new potatoes
400 g can chopped
   tomatoes
1 vegetable stock cube
2 tsp cornflour
142 ml pot soured cream

To garnish:
2 tbsp chopped
   fresh parsley

What you do

1 **Peel** and finely **chop** the onions.

2 Peel and **slice** the carrots and parsnips.

3 Peel the swede and turnip (if using). Cut them into 2 cm thick slices, then into 2 cm chunks.

(!) 4 Heat the oil in a large saucepan. Add the onions and **fry** them for 3 minutes, until softened.

5 Stir in the chopped-up vegetables and paprika, and cook for 5 minutes, stirring from time to time.

6 Sprinkle the flour over the vegetables and cook for 1 minute, stirring all the time.

(!) 7 Pour 300 ml of **boiling** water over the vegetables. Add the new potatoes and canned tomatoes.

8 Crumble the stock cube over the pan and stir well. **Cover** and **simmer** for 25 minutes.

9 In a cup, mix the cornflour with 2 tbsp cold water. Stir the mixture into the soured cream, and then stir the cream into the vegetable mixture.

10 Carefully spoon the hot goulash into a serving dish, and sprinkle with parsley to serve.

Cheese fondue (Switzerland)

Sharing a fondue with friends is a popular Swiss tradition. Everyone takes turns to dip cubes of bread or vegetables into melted cheese in a fondue pan. A small burner under the pan keeps the cheese warm. If you do not have a **fondue set**, gently warm the ingredients in a heavy-based pan over a low heat on the hob. Keep the mixture warm by placing the pan over a heated dish-warmer.

What you need

200 ml grape juice
1 tsp cornflour
1 garlic clove
200 g Gruyère cheese
200 g Emmenthal cheese
1 French loaf (baguette)
4 thick slices rye bread
1 apple
2 tbsp lemon juice
2 carrots

What you do

1 Mix 2 tbsp of the grape juice with the cornflour to make a smooth paste.

2 **Peel** and crush the garlic. Put it into the fondue pan with the cornflour mixture and the rest of the grape juice. Stir well.

3 Cut the rind off both the cheeses. Cut each piece into 1 cm thick slices, then 1 cm wide strips. Now cut the strips into 1 cm cubes.

4 **Slice** the baguette into 2.5 cm slices, then cut each slice into quarters. Cut the rye bread into 3 cm cubes.

5 Cut the apple into eight wedges. Cut out the core and throw it away. Cut the wedges into 2 cm chunks. Put them in a bowl with the lemon juice.

6 Peel the carrots and cut them into 3 cm chunks.

(!) **7** Ask an adult to light the fondue burner. Put the pan on top and let the mixture warm, but not **boil**. Add the cheese, stirring until melted.

8 **Drain** the lemon juice from the apple. Put the apple, bread and carrots on to plates.

9 Give each person a fork (a long fondue fork, if you have them).

10 Each person, in turn, puts a piece of bread, apple or carrot on their fork, dips it into the cheese, stirs the mixture once, takes the fork out and eats! (Take care: the melted cheese will be very hot.)

Vegetable Cornish pasties (England)

Cornwall is in the far south-west of England. These filled pastry envelopes, called pasties, were first made as lunch for miners working deep in the Cornish tin-mines. The men could not wash their hands before eating, so they held a pastry corner as they ate, then threw away the dirty bit. They are ideal as part of a picnic or as a lunch.

What you need

125 g potatoes
125 g carrots
125 g swede
half a vegetable
  stock cube
1 onion
1 tbsp vegetable oil
1 tbsp flour
500 g packet ready-
  made shortcrust
  pastry
1 egg

To garnish:
sprigs of fresh parsley

What you do

1 **Peel** the potatoes, carrots and swede. Cut each into 1 cm slices, then into 1 cm cubes. Put these vegetables into a saucepan, and crumble in half a stock cube.

(!) 2 Cover the vegetables with **boiling** water, bring back to the boil and cook for 10 minutes.

(!) 3 Peel and finely **chop** the onion. Heat the oil in a small pan, and **fry** the onion over a low to medium heat for 4 minutes.

(!) 4 **Drain** the potato, swede and carrots, and then add them to the onion. Leave them to cool completely.

5 **Preheat** the oven to gas mark 6/220 °C/400 °F. Sprinkle the flour on to a work surface. Use a rolling pin to roll the pastry out until it is about 3 mm thick.

6 Put an 18 cm plate on the pastry and cut around it. Repeat this to make six pastry circles.

7 Spoon the vegetables along the centre of each circle. Keep them away from the edge.

8 Brush a little water around the circles' edges. Fold the pastry over the filling. Press the pastry edge between your fingers to make a zig-zag ridge along the edge of each pasty.

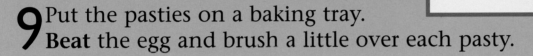

9 Put the pasties on a baking tray. **Beat** the egg and brush a little over each pasty.

10 **Bake** for 25 minutes, until golden. Let the pasties cool a little before eating them, garnished with a sprig of parsley.

Pineapple curry (Sri Lanka)

Sri Lanka is an island in the Indian Ocean, just off the southern tip of India. This recipe uses pineapples and coconuts, two of the island's main crops. It also uses the dried leaves of the curry plant, which add a spicy flavour. Use a heavy-based saucepan for this recipe, if you can. Sri Lankan cooks use a pot called a 'chatty'.

What you need

quarter of a fresh chilli
    (if you like it)
1 tsp mustard seeds
1 shallot
1 large, ripe pineapple
quarter of a stem of
    lemon grass
1 tbsp vegetable oil
3 dried curry leaves
100 ml coconut milk
pinch of saffron
1 small cinnamon stick
½ tsp **ground** cumin

What you do

1 **Chop** the quarter chilli finely (if you are using it), and then wash your hands thoroughly. Chilli juice can make your eyes and skin very sore.

2 Put the mustard seeds into a small frying pan, and **dry-fry** them over a medium heat for 30 seconds, until they 'pop'. Tip them on to a plate.

3 **Peel** and finely chop the shallot.

4 Cut the pineapple in half. Cut off the thick skin and leaves, and throw them away. Cut out the tough core in the middle, and throw it away. Chop the flesh into 2 cm chunks.

5 Peel off the outer leaves off the lemon grass. Trim off the root end and throw it away. Finely chop the lemon grass.

6 Heat the oil in a saucepan over a medium heat. **Fry** the shallot for 1 minute. Add the lemon grass and curry leaves, and fry for 1 minute.

7 Stir in the coconut milk and all the other ingredients, except the ground cumin. **Simmer** for 10 minutes, stirring from time to time.

8 Stir in the cumin, and simmer for 5 minutes. Take the cinnamon out, and serve hot, with rice.

P can pie (USA)

Pecan nuts are an important crop for farmers in the southern USA. They **export** them all over the world. Pecan nuts have a sweeter flavour than most nuts. Pecan pie is a popular traditional dish all over the USA. It is delicious warm or cold.

What you need

50 g dark soft brown sugar
4 tbsp golden syrup
1 tbsp butter
18 cm shortcrust pastry
  flan case
200 g pecan halves
1 egg
1 tsp vanilla essence

What you do

1 Put the sugar, golden syrup and butter into a pan. Heat them very gently over a low heat until the butter has melted. Stir well and leave to cool.

2 **Preheat** the oven to gas mark 4/180 °C/350 °F.

3 Put the pastry case on to a baking sheet.

4 Scatter half the pecans over the pastry, and level them. Arrange a circle of pecan halves around the edge of the pastry, and then another circle inside it. Keep making circles of nuts until you reach the centre.

5 **Beat** the egg and the vanilla essence with a fork. Stir this into the cooled sugar mixture, and then pour the liquid over the pecan nuts.

6 **Bake** the pie for 30 minutes, or until the egg and sugar mixture has set in the centre of the pie. Cool for 15 minutes.

7 Cut the pie into six slices, and serve with ice cream or cream.

THE HISTORY OF PECAN PIE

In the late seventeenth century, French explorers settled in New Orleans, USA. The Native Americans living there introduced them to the pecan nut. The French settlers invented Pecan pie – a delicious way to enjoy the nuts.

Apple pancakes (the Netherlands)

People in the Netherlands enjoy sweet and savoury pancakes. They might cook them with cheese, ham or fruit. Traditionally, Dutch cooks do not roll their pancakes up around the filling. Instead, they cook the filling with the batter, and serve the pancake flat on a large plate. This recipe is a particularly popular one in the Netherlands.

What you need

100 g plain flour
2 tsp soft brown sugar
1 tsp **ground** cinnamon
¼ tsp ground cloves
1 egg
200 ml milk
1 red apple
1 green apple
4 tsp vegetable oil

What you do

1 **Sift** the flour, sugar and ground spices into a bowl. Using your fingers, make a dip in the middle.

2 **Beat** the egg, add the milk and beat until well mixed. Pour the mixture into the dip in the flour, and gradually stir the liquid into the flour.

3 Beat the pancake batter well, and then put it on one side. Turn the oven on to its lowest setting.

4 Use an apple corer to take the apples' cores out.

5 Cut the apples in half, and then into thin **slices**. Stir the apple slices into the batter.

6 Heat ½ tsp oil in an 18 cm frying pan. Using a metal tablespoon, add 2 tablespoons of pancake batter and apple slices to the pan. Tilt the pan to cover the bottom with batter.

7 Cook for 2–3 minutes over a low to medium heat, until the pancake is golden brown on one side.

8 Use a fish slice to flip the pancake over, and cook the other side. Lift the pancake on to a plate, put another plate on top, and keep it warm in the oven while you cook the rest of the batter in the same way.

9 Serve the pancakes hot, either on their own, or with a little golden syrup or ice cream.

Atholl Brose (Scotland)

Atholl Brose means 'broth, or thick soup, from Atholl', which is an area in Scotland. The main ingredients are all produced in Scotland – oatmeal, honey and raspberries. If you prefer, replace the cream with soya cream. Serve as a dessert, or as a cool treat on a hot day.

What you need

6 tbsp pinhead oatmeal
450 ml double cream
3 tbsp runny honey
200 g fresh raspberries
sprigs of mint

What you do

1 Scatter the oatmeal on to a baking tray.

2 Heat the grill to medium. Put the baking tray under the grill, and **grill** the oatmeal for about 1 minute, until the oatmeal starts to turn golden brown. Set it aside to cool.

3 Put the cream into a bowl. Using a hand-held electric whisk or balloon whisk, **whisk** the cream until it starts becoming firmer.

4 Spoon the honey over the cream.

5 Tip the oatmeal into the cream. Using a metal spoon, cut through the cream to **fold** it in.

6 Keeping four raspberries aside, divide the rest up into four glass bowls. Spoon the cream mixture on top of the raspberries.

7 Top each glass with a raspberry and a sprig of fresh mint.

8 **Chill** for 30 minutes before serving.

HEATHERY HONEY

Bees collect pollen from flowers to make into honey. The bees that make Scottish honey have gathered pollen from the heather that covers the hills and mountains of Scotland. Scots say that this makes their honey taste unlike any other kind.

Further information

Here are some places to find out more about vegetarian food and cooking.

Books

Kids Can Cook: Vegetarian Recipes, Dorothy Bates (Book Publishing Company, 2000)
Vegetarian Cooking Around the World, Alison Behnke (Lerner Publishing Company, 2002)
Vegetarian Cooking for Beginners, Fiona Watts (Usborne, 1999)

Websites

www.bbc.co.uk/food/children/feature_vegetarian.shtml
www.bbc.co.uk/food/vegetarian/
www.vegsoc.org/youth/index.html

Conversion chart

Ingredients for recipes can be measured in two different ways. Metric measurements use grams and millilitres. Imperial measurements use ounces and fluid ounces. This book uses metric measurements. The chart here shows you how to convert measurements from metric to imperial.

SOLIDS		LIQUIDS	
METRIC	IMPERIAL	METRIC	IMPERIAL
10 g	¼ oz	30 ml	1 fl oz
15 g	½ oz	50 ml	2 fl oz
25 g	1 oz	75 ml	2½ fl oz
50 g	1¾ oz	100 ml	3½ fl oz
75 g	2¾ oz	125 ml	4 fl oz
100 g	3½ oz	150 ml	5 fl oz
150 g	5 oz	300 ml	10 fl oz
250 g	9 oz	600 ml	20 fl oz
450 g	16 oz		

Healthy eating

This diagram shows which foods you should eat to stay healthy. Most of your food should come from the bottom of the pyramid. Eat some of the foods from the middle every day. Only eat a little of the foods from the top. Although the pyramid recommends meat, being a vegetarian does not mean you cannot eat healthily. Following a balanced vegetarian diet, which provides your body with enough **protein**, is very healthy indeed. Most of the foods we need to stay healthy are in the middle and bottom of this pyramid, which do not include any meat at all. Vegetarians must eat some foods from the top layer as well, such as **pulses**, nuts and milk.

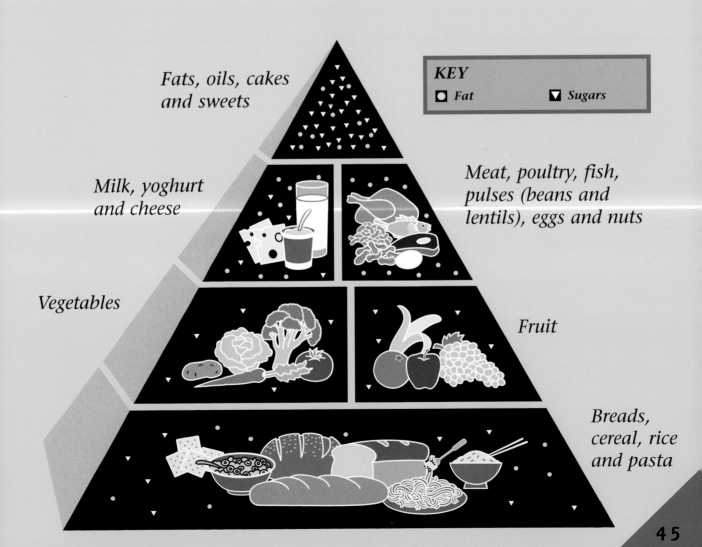

Fats, oils, cakes and sweets

KEY
☐ *Fat*　　　▼ *Sugars*

Milk, yoghurt and cheese

Meat, poultry, fish, pulses (beans and lentils), eggs and nuts

Vegetables

Fruit

Breads, cereal, rice and pasta

Glossary

bake cook something in the oven

beat mix ingredients together strongly, for example, egg yolks and whites

blend mix ingredients together in a blender or food processor

boil cook a liquid on the hob. Boiling liquid bubbles and steams strongly.

calcium mineral in foods, such as milk and cheese, that helps us have strong teeth and bones

chill put a dish into the fridge for a while

chop cut into pieces using a sharp knife

chutney a spicy sauce served with curries. Chutneys often contain chopped fruit and vegetables.

cover put a lid on a pan, or put foil or clingfilm over a dish

deep-fry cook in a deep pan of hot oil

drain remove liquid, usually by pouring something into a colander or sieve

dressing oil and vinegar sauce for salad

dry-fry fry in a pan without any oil

export to sell a product, such as fruit, to another country

fold mixing wet and dry ingredients by making cutting movements with a metal spoon

fondue set utensils used for melting cheese

fry cook something in oil in a pan

grate break something, such as cheese, into small pieces using a grater

grill cook under a grill

ground made into a fine powder

knead mix ingredients into a smooth dough for bread

mash crush a food until it is soft and pulpy

nutrient substance that provides nourishment

peel remove the skin of a fruit or vegetable

pitta bread flat, unrisen bread

preheat turn on the oven in advance, so that it is hot when you want to use it

protein a natural substance in food that our bodies need to stay healthy

pulse beans, peas or seeds from plants that often have pods

sift pass through a sieve

simmer cook liquid on the hob. Simmering liquid bubbles and steams gently.

slice cut into thin flat pieces

staple one of the most important foods in a person's diet is called a staple food

thawed no longer frozen

toast heat under a grill or in a toaster

vegan person who does not eat any food that has come from an animal, including milk and eggs

vegetarian food that does not contain meat. People who do not eat meat are called vegetarians.

vitamins natural chemicals in food that the body uses to stay healthy

whisk mix ingredients using a whisk

Index

6696670R00061

Printed in Germany
by Amazon Distribution
GmbH, Leipzig

First published in 2014 by
Clarity Media Ltd
www.clarity-media.co.uk

D0185539

Puzzles created by Dan Moore
Design and layout by Amy Smith

About Clarity Media

Clarity Media are a leading provider of a huge range of puzzles for adults and children. For more information on our services, please visit us at www. pzle.co.uk. For information on purchasing puzzles for publication, visit us at www.clarity-media.co.uk

Puzzle Magazines

If you enjoy the puzzles in this book, then you may be interested in our puzzle magazines. We have a very large range of magazines that you can download and print yourself in PDF format at our Puzzle Magazine site. For more information, take a look
at http://www.puzzle-magazine.com

Online Puzzles

If you prefer to play puzzles online, please take a look at the Puzzle Club website, at
www.thepuzzleclub.com

**We also have more puzzle books available at
www.puzzle-book.co.uk**

Contents

Half-Alpha Crossword

In these crosswords all your answers must only contain letters from the first half of the alphabet, as listed underneath each puzzle. The letters N – Z must not appear in a single one of your answers!

Jigsaw Crossword

The solution grid has been split into small pieces. You must work out where each piece goes in the grid to solve the puzzle and reveal the completed crossword grid. Each piece is used exactly once. The clues are given to help you solve the puzzle.

Ladder Crossword

Can you fill the letter ladder by solving all the standard crossword clues?

Just The Once Crossword

There are 26 clues in this crossword variant, and the answers start with each of the letters A – Z exactly once. So if you place the word 'Example' as one of your answers, no other answer can start with the letter 'E', and so on. The across and down clues for the puzzle are given, but in random order, so you'll need to work out where each answer fits in the grid to solve the puzzle.

Word Square

Word squares are mini 4 x 4 crossword puzzles with a fun twist – the answers are the same in both the across and down direction!

Pangram Crossword

A pangram is a standard crossword puzzle, but it must contain each letter from A – Z one or more times. A cross-out letter grid is given underneath the puzzle so you can record which letters you've used.

Star Letter Crossword

These are ordinary crossword puzzles but with a twist: each puzzle has a 'star letter' that must appear at least once in every single one of your answers. The star letter is given at the start of each puzzle.

Triplet Crossword

In these puzzles all answers must start with one of three letters that are given at the top of each puzzle. For instance, if the puzzle is 'ABC Triplet' then all answers must start with either A, B or C.

Anagram Crossword

All the clues in these puzzles are anagrams of the answers: sometimes there will be more than one possible anagram of a series of letters so you'll need to cross-reference other answers in the grid to find the correct anagram to fill the grid.

A-Z Puzzles

Each letter of the alphabet from A – Z has been removed from the grid once, to leave 26 empty circled squares. You must work out which letter from A – Z fits in each of the blank circles and write it in, so as to fill the crossword grid and solve the puzzle.

Double Definition

A double definition crossword is a standard crossword puzzle, but each clue contains not one but two definitions for each answer word.

Every Letter Counts

In these mini-crosswords you are given a list of letters that each appear just once in the grid. You must solve the crossword clues using each letter from the list a single time – every letter really does count!

4

Skeleton Crossword

With a skeleton crossword you not only need to solve the clues to fill the grid but also build the grid at the same time. Each grid exhibits standard 180 degree rotational symmetry. Some starter numbers and blank cells are given to get you started. Use this information along with the clues and the grid symmetry to solve the puzzle and complete the grid. Good luck!

Spiral Crossword

In a spiral crossword you start at the top left and work your way clockwise around the grid until you reach the central square. The last letter of an answer is shared with the first letter of the next answer. Two other words will appear in the grey diagonals once the grid is complete.

Vowelless Crossword

The clues for vowelless crosswords are the answer words – but without any of their vowels! For instance the clue 'FT' could be answered with 'FAT' or 'FIT'. You'll need to use your vocabulary and knowledge of the English language to work out the possible words that can fit each letter pattern, together with the other answers in the grid to work out which option must be placed where there is more than one possible matching word.

Good Luck & Happy Solving!

Across

1 - Country in southern Asia (5)

4 - Person of high rank (7)

7 - Wander off track (5)

8 - Group of spectators (8)

9 - Equipped (5)

11 - Parroted (anag) (8)

15 - And so on (2,6)

17 - Gain knowledge (5)

19 - Hindered (8)

20 - Make a sound expressing pain (5)

21 - Characteristics (7)

22 - Chopping (5)

Down

1 - Fair (9)

2 - Deliberately impassive (7)

3 - Is present at (7)

4 - South American cowboy (6)

5 - Character of a person (6)

6 - Fill with high spirits (5)

10 - Requiring much skill (of a task) (9)

12 - Part of the ocean (4,3)

13 - Italian fast racing car (7)

14 - Refined in manner (6)

16 - Short written works (6)

18 - British noblemen (5)

Across

7 - Money lent to publicly acknowledge (6)

8 - Snooker ball shade (6)

10 - Drug unlikely to cause offence (7)

11 - Furniture to put a motion forward (5)

12 - Program cipher (4)

13 - Comic party (5)

17 - Ornament to delight greatly (5)

18 - Trotter to pay the bill (4)

22 - Discard rubbish (5)

23 - One with innate talent, not synthetic (7)

24 - Reprimand to increase rapidly (6)

25 - Expert prophet (6)

Down

1 - Cancel score (7)

2 - Backs brief moments (7)

3 - Plastic record (5)

4 - Happy innards (7)

5 - Idiot bird (5)

6 - Command organisation (5)

9 - Foreign or outlandish falcon (9)

14 - Axe helicopter (7)

15 - Counteract right (7)

16 - Stopped running and ceased making progress (7)

19 - Operators - those who exploit others (5)

20 - Stunt fool (5)

21 - Begin twitch (5)

A B C D E F G H I J K L M N O P Q R S T U V W X Y Z

Across

1 - Rounded mass of steamed dough (8)

6 - Consumes (4)

8 - Willow twigs (6)

9 - Keyboard instruments (6)

10 - In what way (3)

11 - True information (4)

12 - Ten more than eighty (6)

13 - Reformulate (6)

15 - Utterly senseless (6)

17 - Lizard (6)

20 - Joke (4)

21 - Bleat of a sheep (3)

22 - Structures or models (6)

23 - The flowing back of a liquid (6)

24 - Sleepy (4)

25 - Stocky (8)

Down

2 - Upmarket (7)

3 - Crimp (5)

4 - Towards the coast (7)

5 - Adult (5)

6 - Motors (7)

7 - Religious doctrine (5)

14 - Idiotically (7)

15 - Fish tanks (7)

16 - Ecstatic joy (7)

18 - Lizard (5)

19 - Embarrass (5)

20 - Short time (5)

(grid with numbers 7, 12, 13)

Across

1 - Eg Iceland

4 - Norway lobsters

9 - Inactive pill

10 - Open-meshed material

11 - Makes musical sounds

12 - Parts in a play

14 - Wound the pride of

15 - Cylinder of smoking tobacco

17 - Go inside

18 - Natural environment

20 - Measure of how pressing something is

21 - Patterns

22 - Ranked based on merit

Down

1 - Enforce compliance with

2 - Discovering; finding out

3 - Requirements

5 - Apprehend; snare

6 - The south of France

7 - Pictures

8 - An argument that does not follow

13 - Heard

14 - Imaginary

15 - Roman military unit

16 - Made a victim of

17 - Keen

19 - Computer memory unit

S	U	○	T	L	E	T	○	■	A	○	E	○
■	P	■	R	■	○	■	E	S	■	S	■	○
A	○	O	○	T	I	■	A	N	S	○	E	R
■	○	■	C	■	N	O	R	■	A	■	N	■
H	A	○	○	■	○	■	S	U	A	S	■	○
■	D	■	■	■	○	■	■	L	■	■	■	■
○	E	R	R	E	T	■	L	○	T	E	S	T
■	E	■	■	■	■	■	U	■	■	■	I	■
○	O	G	○	A	M	■	L	○	■	I	Z	E
■	R	■	○	■	E	E	L	■	T	■	○	■
L	I	A	○	S	E	■	A	F	I	E	L	D
■	B	■	N	■	○	■	B	■	L	■	E	■
Z	I	○	S	■	S	P	Y	G	L	A	S	S

A B C D E F G H I J K L M N O P Q R S T U V W X Y Z

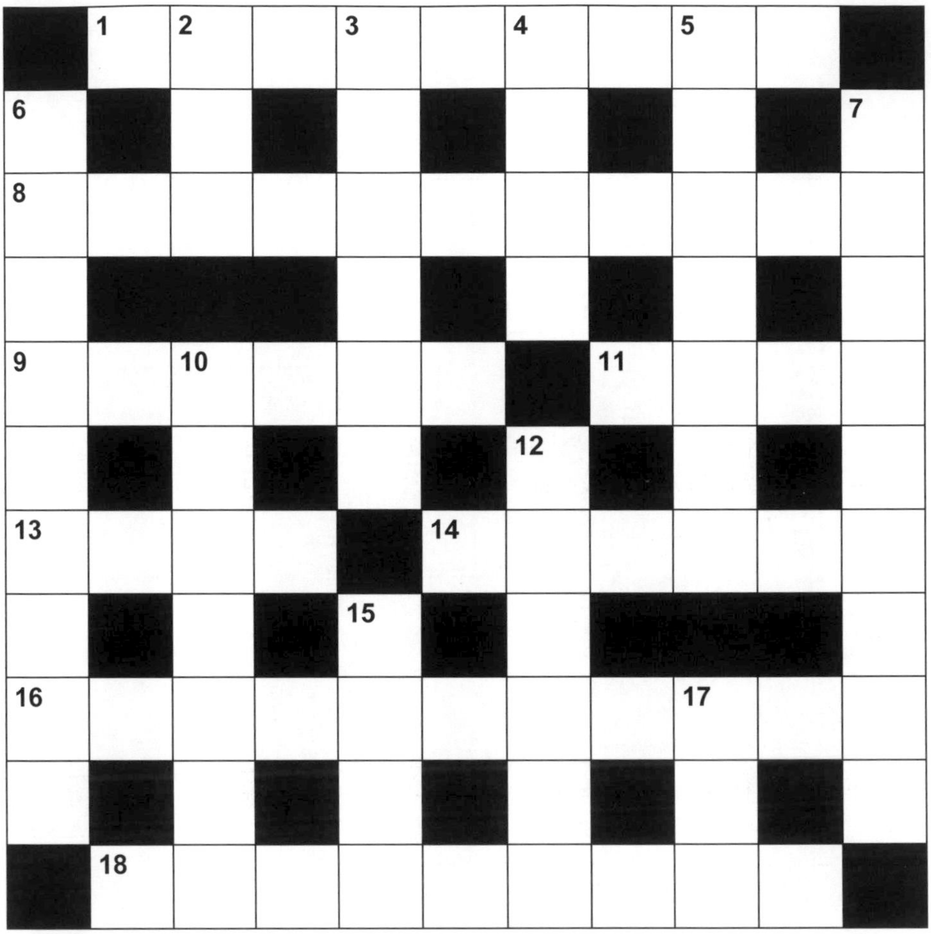

Across

1 - RJNDR

8 - TMPRTR

9 - NTTL

11 - FR

13 - XD

14 - RNWS

16 - DSTRCTV

18 - NBNDD

Down

2 - LM

3 - PNLY

4 - NR

5 - MLT

6 - STNDRDS

7 - DPRSSD

10 - TRSN

12 - DCN

15 - TR

17 - R

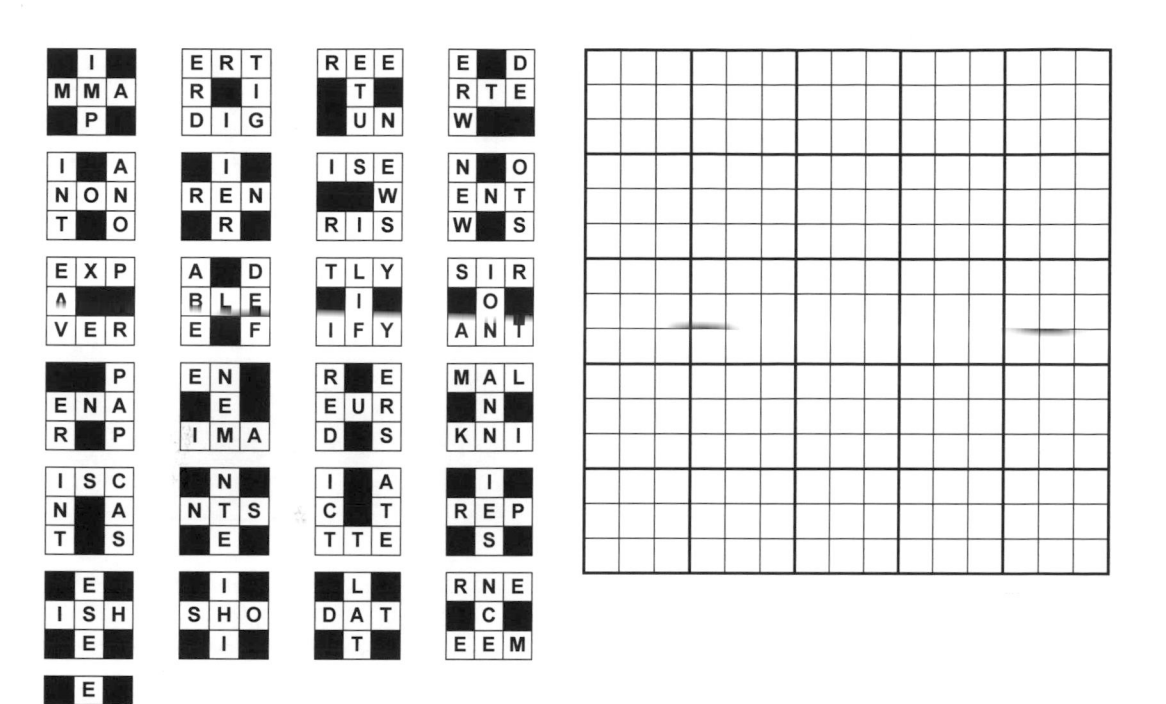

Can you slot the jigsaw pieces into the grid correctly, to create a completed crossword? Use the clues we have listed below to help you out. The grid exhibits standard crossword grid symmetry.

Across

1 - Country where one finds Bamako (4)

9 - Not catching fire easily (3-9)

10 - Make a garment using wool (4)

11 - Circumspectly (10)

15 - Lessen (7)

16 - Bring together (5)

18 - Skill (9)

19 - Statistics and facts (4)

20 - Express a desire for (4)

21 - Green patina formed on copper (9)

23 - Warning noise from an emergency vehicle (5)

24 - People who rent property (7)

26 - Eg positrons (10)

29 - Sea eagle (4)

30 - Someone who sets up their own business (12)

31 - Appear to be (4)

Down

2 - Total destruction (12)

3 - Entwine (10)

4 - Positive electrode (5)

5 - Trees of the genus Ulmus (4)

6 - Momentum (7)

7 - Encourage in wrongdoing (4)

8 - Openly refuse to obey an order (4)

12 - Forbid (9)

13 - Reprimand severely (9)

14 - Jail term without end (4,8)

17 - Daily periodicals (10)

22 - Foes (7)

25 - Made a mistake (5)

26 - Once more (4)

27 - Small children (4)

28 - Row or level of a structure (4)

Across

7 - Frozen water spear (6)

8 - Packed (6)

10 - Brazilian dance (7)

11 - ___ Izzard: stand-up comedian (5)

12 - Every (4)

13 - Third Greek letter (5)

17 - In front (5)

18 - Bivalve marine mollusc (4)

22 - Sweet-scented shrub (5)

23 - Forbidden by law (7)

24 - Moved at an easy pace (6)

25 - Stout-bodied insect (6)

Down

1 - Dealt with a tough question (7)

2 - Novelty (7)

3 - Epic poem ascribed to Homer (5)

4 - Difficult choice (7)

5 - Edge of a knife (5)

6 - Summed together (5)

9 - Tree known for the nut it produces (9)

14 - Verified (7)

15 - Mournful (7)

16 - Mercury alloy (7)

19 - Simple aquatic plants (5)

20 - Church farmland (5)

21 - Threshing tool (5)

9 Every Letter Counts

Across

1 - ___ in: eat heartily (4)

3 - Hogs (4)

Down

1 - Confine; snare (4)

2 - Items that unlock doors (4)

A C E G I K

P R S T U Y

10 Ladder Crossword

Across

3 - Impel; spur on (4)

4 - Mongrel dog (4)

5 - Robert De ___ : actor (4)

6 - Adolescent (abbrev) (4)

7 - ___ Sharif: Egyptian actor (4)

Down

1 - Highest point (11)

2 - Region including Cornwall and Devon (4,7)

14

Across

7 - On a ship or train (6)

8 - Subsidiary action (6)

10 - Light beard (7)

11 - ___ gas: eg neon or argon (5)

12 - Comply (4)

13 - Pierces (5)

17 - Facial hair (5)

18 - Robe (anag) (4)

22 - Seventh sign of the zodiac (5)

23 - Slanting (7)

24 - Insect of the order Coleoptera (6)

25 - Physical item (6)

Down

1 - Double-reed instrument (7)

2 - Payments in addition to wages (7)

3 - Babies' beds (5)

4 - Eventually (2,3,2)

5 - Church farmland (5)

6 - Computer memory units (5)

9 - Mail slot (6,3)

14 - Plausible; defensible (7)

15 - Bunch of flowers (7)

16 - Below (7)

19 - Bludgeons (5)

20 - Henrik ___ : Norwegian author (5)

21 - Excuse of any kind (5)

E		I		B			E		C		P
M	I	S	H	A	○		E	X	U	L	T	S
B		○		N		○		P		I		○
A	L	L	E	G	R	O		A	○	F	○	L
R		A		S		N		N		○		M
○	○	T	H		A	S	I	D	○			
S		E		P		T		S		○		○
			○	O	C	A	L		H	A	○	O
G		U		S		N		F		○		S
U	P	S	E	○		C	R	O	○	U	E	T
T		I		○		○				A		E
○	Y	N	T	A	X		○		E	○		A	S
Y		G		○			○			S		S

A B C D E F G H I J K L M N O P Q R S T U V W X Y Z

Across

7 - Continent (6)

8 - Conclude (6)

10 - Confine (7)

11 - Angry (5)

12 - Chopped (4)

13 - Acknowledged; assumed (5)

17 - Additional payment for good performance (5)

18 - Tool (4)

22 - Forelock of hair (5)

23 - Page templates (7)

24 - Urges to act (6)

25 - Side to side movement (6)

Down

1 - Polish (7)

2 - More important (7)

3 - Prickly (5)

4 - Says out loud (7)

5 - Pertaining to the moon (5)

6 - Hand tool (5)

9 - Gravely (9)

14 - Light fluffy dish (7)

15 - Declare to be (7)

16 - Restrained (7)

19 - Furnish or supply (5)

20 - Slips (anag) (5)

21 - Verse form (5)

Across

1 - Very busy and full

9 - Became less intense

10 - Level golf score

11 - Aimed (anag)

12 - ___ Dushku: US actress

13 - Disregards

16 - Approximate

18 - Opposite of lows

21 - Suffuse with colour

22 - Part of a pen

23 - Undo a knot

24 - Sent back to one's own country

Down

2 - Sausages in bread rolls

3 - Declare (anag)

4 - Support; help

5 - Shelf

6 - Island in the Bay of Naples

7 - Becoming less

8 - Rent manager (anag)

14 - Mediterranean resort area

15 - Cab ride (anag)

17 - Stationary part of a motor

19 - Triangular wall part

20 - Small room used as a steam bath

Across

A fact that has been verified (5)

A ball game (5)

Series of linked metal rings (5)

Ox-like mammals (4)

Striped animal (5)

Remove goods from a van (6)

Cry of derision (4)

Wild horse (6)

___ Moore: Hollywood actress (4)

Ancient Persian king (6)

Utilise wrongly (6)

Catch sight of (4)

Down

Sharp chopping implement (3)

Risky undertaking (7)

Smiles contemptuously (6)

Alumnus of a public school (3,3)

Child who has no home (4)

Area of a church (4)

Platform leading out to sea (4)

Large lizard (6)

Ask questions (4)

Come together (3)

Set of instructions (6)

Foot of a horse (4)

Caustic calcium compound (4)

Form of singing for entertainment (7)

Across

7 - Seek to hurt (6)

8 - Next to (6)

10 - United States (7)

11 - ___ Adkins: singer (5)

12 - Mountain system in Europe (4)

13 - Starting point (5)

17 - Obscure road (5)

18 - Bay (4)

22 - Excuse of any kind (5)

23 - Upset; affect (7)

24 - Item of neckwear (6)

25 - Evoke a feeling (6)

Down

1 - Yellow fruits (7)

2 - Try (7)

3 - Bitterly pungent (5)

4 - Made of clay hardened by heat (7)

5 - Alcoholic beverage (5)

6 - Beets (anag) (5)

9 - Boat (9)

14 - Sceptical (7)

15 - Abundant (7)

16 - Insects with biting mouthparts (7)

19 - Group of goods produced at one time (5)

20 - Cylinder of smoking tobacco (5)

21 - Burning (5)

Across

1 - PAARCACE

6 - THTIG

7 - TIRSP

9 - ERWE

10 - LKTREI

12 - ANYMAL

14 - WKSE

17 - ABSAM

18 - GNOLA

19 - TOSEISNI

Down

2 - LGEAA

3 - CSTA

4 - ASSLAI

5 - GTEER

6 - TSLREIL

8 - RGPWEII

11 - AIASFR

13 - ENYEM

15 - NTKSO

16 - LMIA

18 Spiral Crossword

The last letter of each answer will become the first letter of the next answer.
Two other words will appear in the grey diagonals.

1 - With hands on the hips
2 - Sets of six balls (cricket)
3 - Poor handwriting
4 - Relay (anag)
5 - Exposes to danger
6 - Reigns (anag)
7 - Appreciates
8 - Majestic
9 - Children
10 - Lure
11 - Amended
12 - Danes (anag)
13 - Thick drink
14 - Background actors
15 - Grain store
16 - Upon

19 Word Square

Aromatic herb

Suggestion

Tax

Puts down

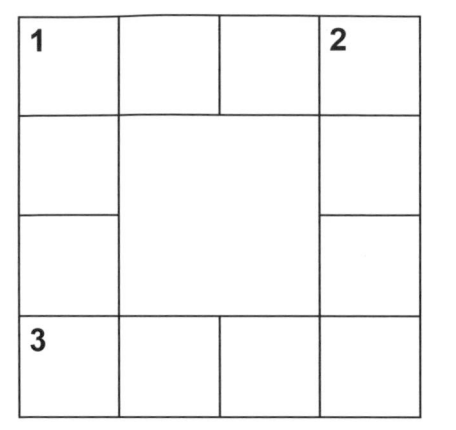

A B E G I K
L N O R U W

Across

1 - Male monarch (4)

3 - Send down a ball in cricket (4)

Down

1 - Pavement edge (4)

2 - Ancient France (4)

Across

3 - Abominable snowman (4)

4 - Circular storage medium (4)

5 - Domestic cattle (4)

6 - Hired form of transport (4)

7 - Unwrap (4)

Down

1 - Act of publishing content in several places (11)

2 - Debates (11)

Across

1 - Unit of linear measure (4)

3 - Explicit and clearly stated (8)

9 - Former Greek monetary unit (7)

10 - Capital of Ghana (5)

11 - Go away from quickly (5)

12 - Bodies of writing (7)

13 - Pull back from (6)

15 - Form-fitting garment (6)

17 - Emotional stability (7)

18 - Performer (5)

20 - Cluster (5)

21 - Fragrant compound (7)

22 - Overshadows (8)

23 - Great tennis serves (4)

Down

1 - Incapable of being expressed in words (13)

2 - Lead a discussion (5)

4 - Flatfish (6)

5 - Ability to see the future (12)

6 - Influences that contribute to a result (7)

7 - Dull and uninteresting (13)

8 - Type of contest (12)

14 - Army rank (7)

16 - Determine (6)

19 - Uniform jacket (5)

A B C D E F G H I J K L M N O P Q R S T U V W X Y Z

A B C D E F G H I J K L M N O P Q R S T U V W X Y Z

Across

1 - Mexican cloak (6)

7 - Liable to error (8)

8 - Knock vigorously (3)

9 - Common bird (6)

10 - Relocate (4)

11 - Marsh plant (5)

13 - Act of putting pen to paper (7)

15 - Rubbed (7)

17 - Nerve (5)

21 - Republic in W Africa (4)

22 - Turning force (6)

23 - One who steers boats (3)

24 - Outlines (8)

25 - Individual (6)

Down

1 - Money pouches (6)

2 - Seized with teeth (6)

3 - Many times (5)

4 - Complete (7)

5 - Inconsistency (8)

6 - Number in soccer team (6)

12 - Cover with ice (8)

14 - Enthusiastic (7)

16 - Writing implement (6)

18 - Expels (6)

19 - Horn (6)

20 - Understand (5)

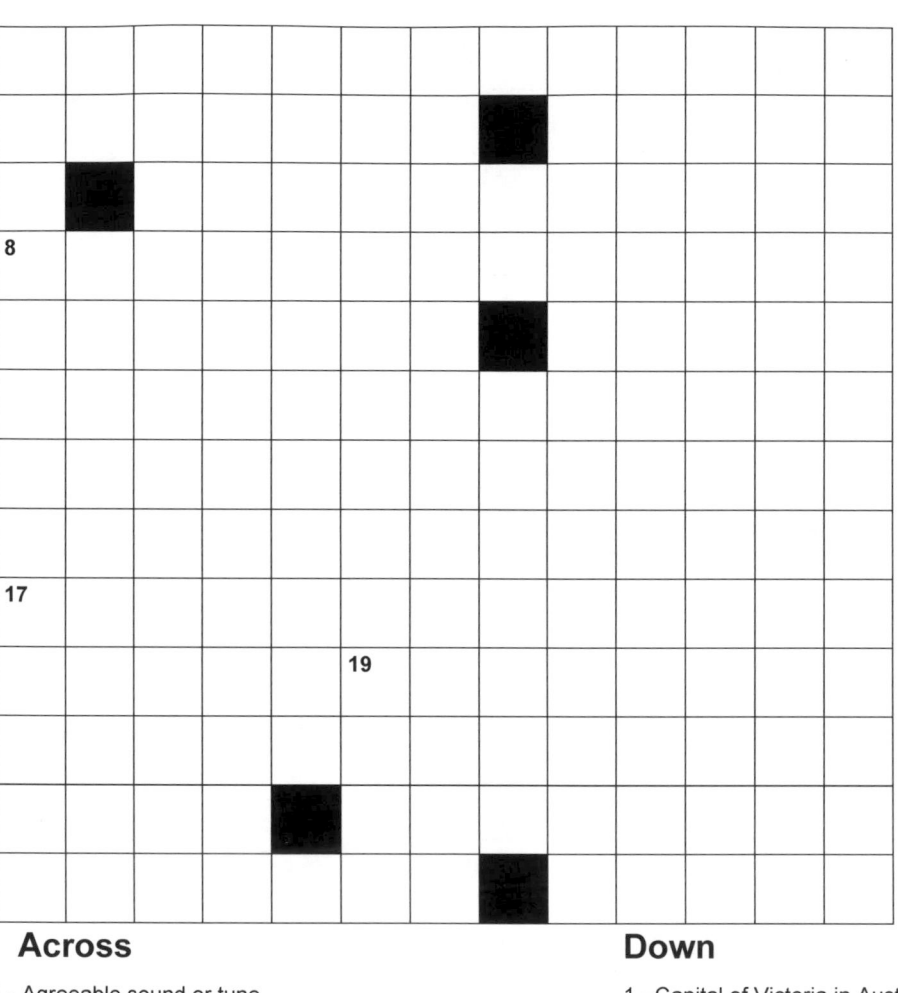

Across

1 - Agreeable sound or tune

4 - Wealthy

7 - Liquid measure

8 - Inhales

9 - Stretched tight (of a muscle)

11 - Unproven

15 - Hamper

17 - Sea duck

19 - Assimilate again

20 - Behaved

21 - Walked upon

22 - Blowing in puffs (of wind)

Down

1 - Capital of Victoria in Australia

2 - Next after sixth

3 - Dispute or competition

4 - Respire with difficulty

5 - Less quiet

6 - Blazes

10 - All people

12 - Massaging

13 - Elongated rectangles

14 - Fable

16 - Liam ___ : Schindler's List actor

18 - Bring on oneself

26 Vowelless Crossword

Across

1 - BRLLNT

6 - BPD

8 - RLC

9 - SWM

10 - MRGN

12 - TRWL

13 - PLM

15 - PCH

16 - SHS

17 - SDSHWS

Down

1 - BBYSTTR

2 - LDY

3 - RBG

4 - TLGRPH

5 - CNMSTS

7 - PSNS

11 - MTHD

14 - LGS

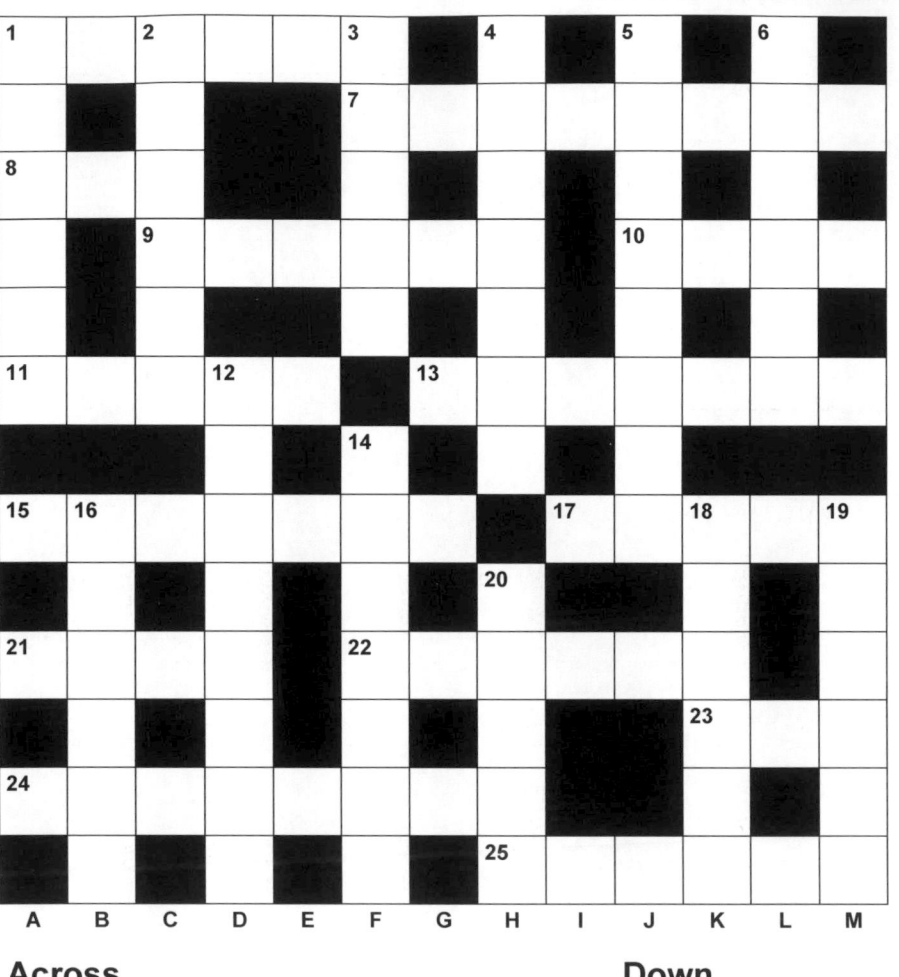

Across

1 - Spiny tree or shrub (6)

7 - Worrying problem (8)

8 - Not well (3)

9 - Opposite of an acid (6)

10 - Fine open fabric (4)

11 - Impertinence (5)

13 - Knight of King Arthur (7)

15 - Mark written under the letter c (7)

17 - Assumed proposition (5)

21 - The south of France (4)

22 - Soothed (6)

23 - Frozen water (3)

24 - Summon to return (4,4)

25 - Symbol or representation (6)

Down

1 - Sour to the taste (6)

2 - Ablaze (6)

3 - In front (5)

4 - Enchanting (7)

5 - Eg rugby or tennis (4,4)

6 - Modern ballroom dance (3-3)

12 - Qualified for entry (8)

14 - Extremely cold (7)

16 - ___ Wood: US actor (6)

18 - Positioned in the middle (6)

19 - Shining (6)

20 - Individual piece of snow (5)

28 Word Square

Playthings

Unwrap

Abominable snowman

Cut

29 Word Square

Cuts the grass

Quartz-like gem

Pottery

Turn or slide violently (of a vehicle)

Across

1 - Homeless person (4)

3 - Has to (4)

Down

1 - Computer virus (4)

2 - Touched (4)

A E F I L M
O R S T U W

Across

3 - Talk wildly (4)

4 - Wizard (4)

5 - Roman Emperor (4)

6 - Mischievous god in Norse mythology (4)

7 - Spiritual teacher (4)

Down

1 - Study of lawbreaking (11)

2 - Overly polite (11)

Across

1 - Stage plays (6)

4 - Worshipped (6)

9 - Walked upon (7)

10 - Medical practitioners (7)

11 - Quoted (5)

12 - Rafael ___ : Spanish tennis star (5)

14 - Old-fashioned (5)

15 - Wild dog of Australia (5)

17 - Nadir (anag) (5)

18 - Submarine weapon (7)

20 - Relaxed (7)

21 - Annoying person (6)

22 - Organs that secrete (6)

Down

1 - Disengage (6)

2 - Take up of a practice (8)

3 - Assisted (5)

5 - Move downwards (7)

6 - Repeat (4)

7 - Type of engine (6)

8 - Diligent (11)

13 - Decline in activity (8)

14 - Mournful (7)

15 - Adoring (6)

16 - Classifies; sorts (6)

17 - Lowed (anag) (5)

19 - Kevin ___ : former Australian Prime Minister (4)

A B C D E F G H I J K L M N O P Q R S T U V W X Y Z

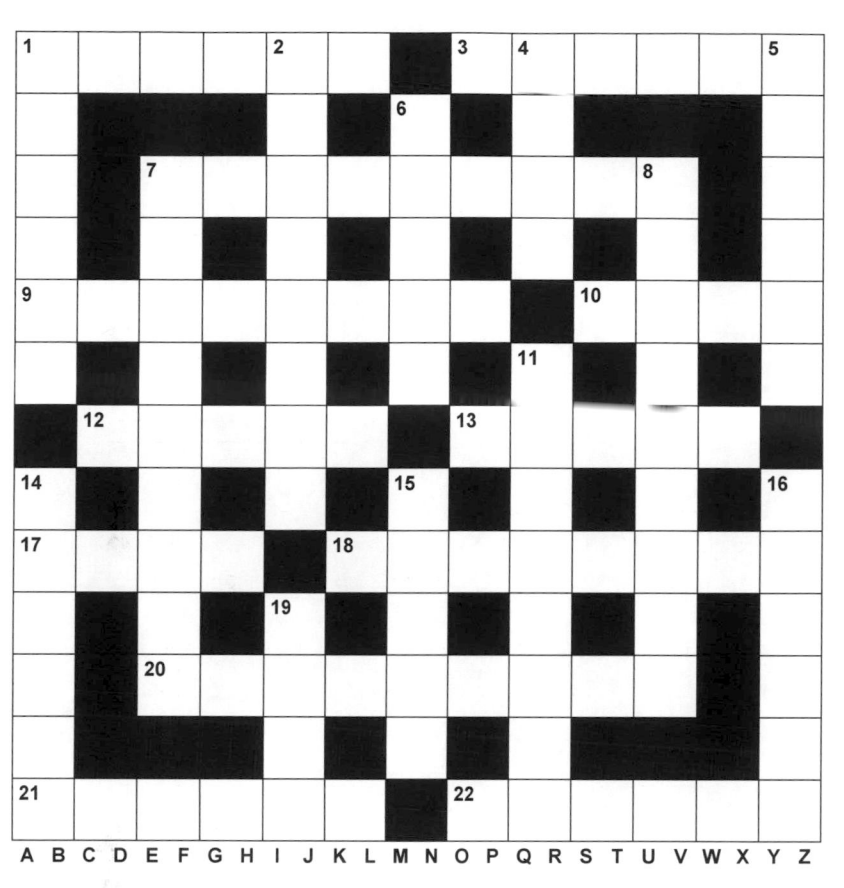

Across

1 - No one (6)

3 - Striped animals (6)

7 - Staying (9)

9 - Compassion (8)

10 - Canine tooth (4)

12 - Links wool together (5)

13 - Crawl (5)

17 - Dispatched (4)

18 - Renounce under oath (8)

20 - Decade from 1970 - 1979 (9)

21 - Parrot sound (6)

22 - Burn (6)

Down

1 - Immature water insects (6)

2 - Control (8)

4 - Depart from (4)

5 - Miserly (6)

6 - Elevators (5)

7 - Cud chewing animals (9)

8 - Inelegant (9)

11 - Having faith in (8)

14 - Incidental remarks; stage whispers (6)

15 - Articulation; shared by two or more (5)

16 - ___ jump: event in athletics (6)

19 - Affirm solemnly (4)

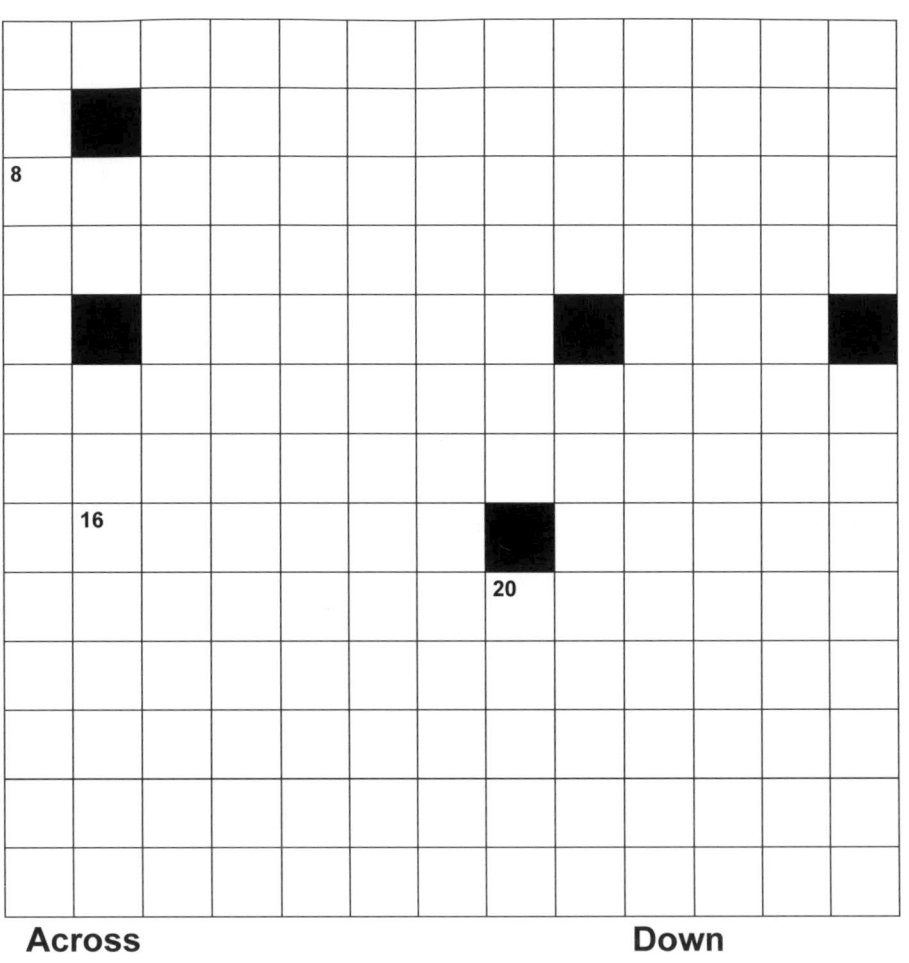

Across

1 - Long mountain chain

7 - Feigns

8 - Grassland

9 - Spinal (anag)

10 - Travel on water

11 - Rushes

13 - Safe places

15 - Report of an event

17 - Dark brown colour

21 - Jar lids

22 - The words of a song

23 - One and one

24 - Bleak; stark

25 - Small finch

Down

1 - Tray

2 - Pass (of time)

3 - Small insect

4 - Restrained

5 - Restore confidence to

6 - Value; respect

12 - Wedge to keep an entrance open

14 - Reveal

16 - Enclosed recess

18 - Points (anag)

19 - Nimble

20 - Type of porridge

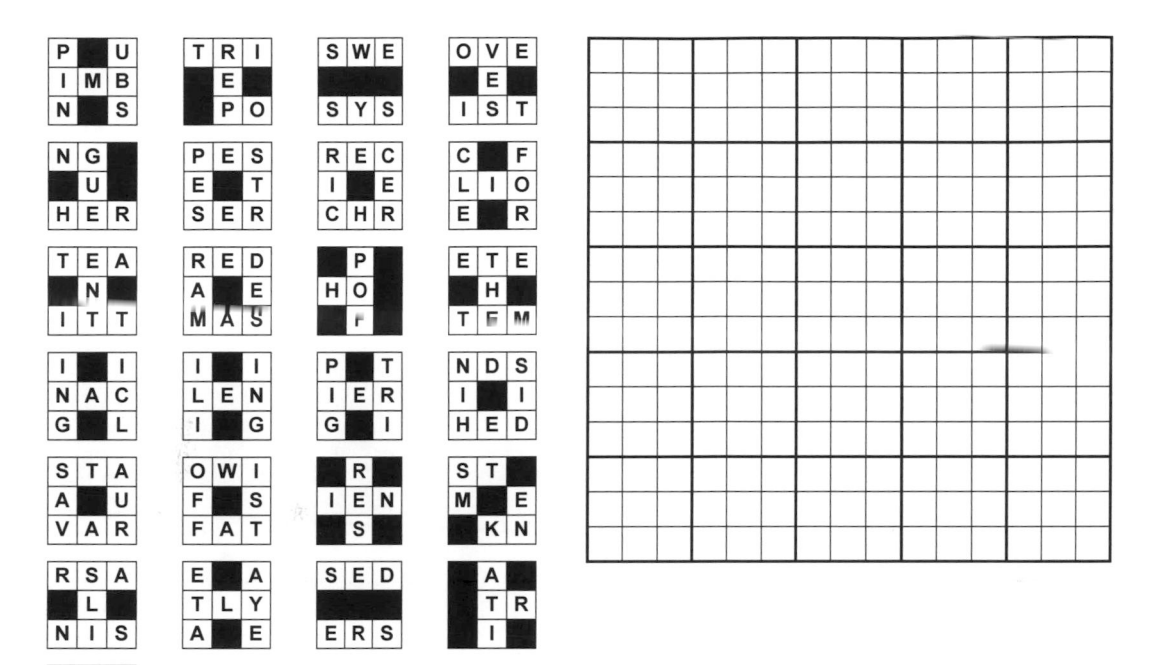

Can you slot the jigsaw pieces into the grid correctly, to create a completed crossword? Use the clues we have listed below to help you out. The grid exhibits standard crossword grid symmetry.

Across

1 - The US flag (5,3,7)

9 - Coated (9)

10 - Show-off (5)

11 - Tortilla topped with cheese (5)

12 - Mercifully (9)

13 - Most saccharine (8)

14 - Made fun of someone (6)

16 - A complex whole (6)

18 - Trinkets (anag) (8)

22 - Very confused situation (9)

23 - One who always puts in a lot of effort (5)

24 - Outstanding (of a debt) (5)

25 - Regained one's strength (9)

26 - Santa Claus (6,9)

Down

1 - Money put aside for the future (7)

2 - Structure resembling an ear (7)

3 - Small mistake in speech (4,2,3,6)

4 - Extreme form of scepticism (8)

5 - Short track for storing trains (6)

6 - Agents (15)

7 - Old Spanish currency (pl) (7)

8 - Moved away from the right course (7)

15 - Confrere (anag) (8)

16 - Incidental result of a larger project (4-3)

17 - Remain alive (7)

19 - Witty saying (7)

20 - Walks with long steps (7)

21 - Religious leader (6)

Across

7 - Avoided (6)

8 - Breathe out (6)

10 - Make amends (7)

11 - Consumed (of food) (5)

12 - Repudiate (4)

13 - Military constructions (5)

17 - ___ Izzard: stand-up comedian (5)

18 - Plant with fronds (4)

22 - Style of Greek architecture (5)

23 - Oval shape (7)

24 - Spirited (6)

25 - Portray (6)

Down

1 - Relies upon (7)

2 - Curbing (7)

3 - Decomposition (5)

4 - Anticipates (7)

5 - Indoor game (5)

6 - Tactical manoeuvre (5)

9 - Placed money in the bank (9)

14 - Instruct (7)

15 - Feeling of hopelessness (7)

16 - Friendly understanding (7)

19 - Enlighten; educate morally (5)

20 - ___ Els: golfing star (5)

21 - ___ DeGeneres: US comedienne (5)

38 Anagram Crossword

Across

1 - MLESODEMED

5 - RMUUD

7 - AADPN

9 - MLEOYD

10 - TAHU

12 - PSIG

13 - ETAREP

16 - OEDRE

17 - HENSE

18 - OOANRMSCIT

Down

1 - MOEDM

2 - MLADAB

3 - ASSP

4 - ORETNOMME

6 - GINELOSRI

8 - SHA

11 - NOASSE

12 - IPE

14 - TCNOI

15 - GAER

The last letter of each answer will become the first letter of the next answer.
Two other words will appear in the grey diagonals.

1 - Cheeky
2 - Taut
3 - Day of the week
4 - Screaming
5 - Unselfish
6 - Repast
7 - Destiny; fate
8 - Instrument for determining height
9 - Denier (anag)
10 - Small inflatable boat
11 - Servant in a royal household
12 - Food
13 - Female relation
14 - Gives out
15 - Male teacher

Reduces in length

___ Major: the Great Bear

Russian sovereign

Indian garment

41 Every Letter Counts

Across

1 - Female domestic helper (4)

3 - Extravagant publicity (4)

Down

1 Sentimentality (4)

2 - Slumber (4)

A D E H I M

O P S U Y Z

42 Ladder Crossword

Across

3 - Wicked (4)

4 - Formal dance (4)

5 - Where a bird lays eggs (4)

6 - Image of a god (4)

7 - Opposite of short (4)

Down

1 - Trustworthy (11)

2 - Act gloomily (anag) (11)

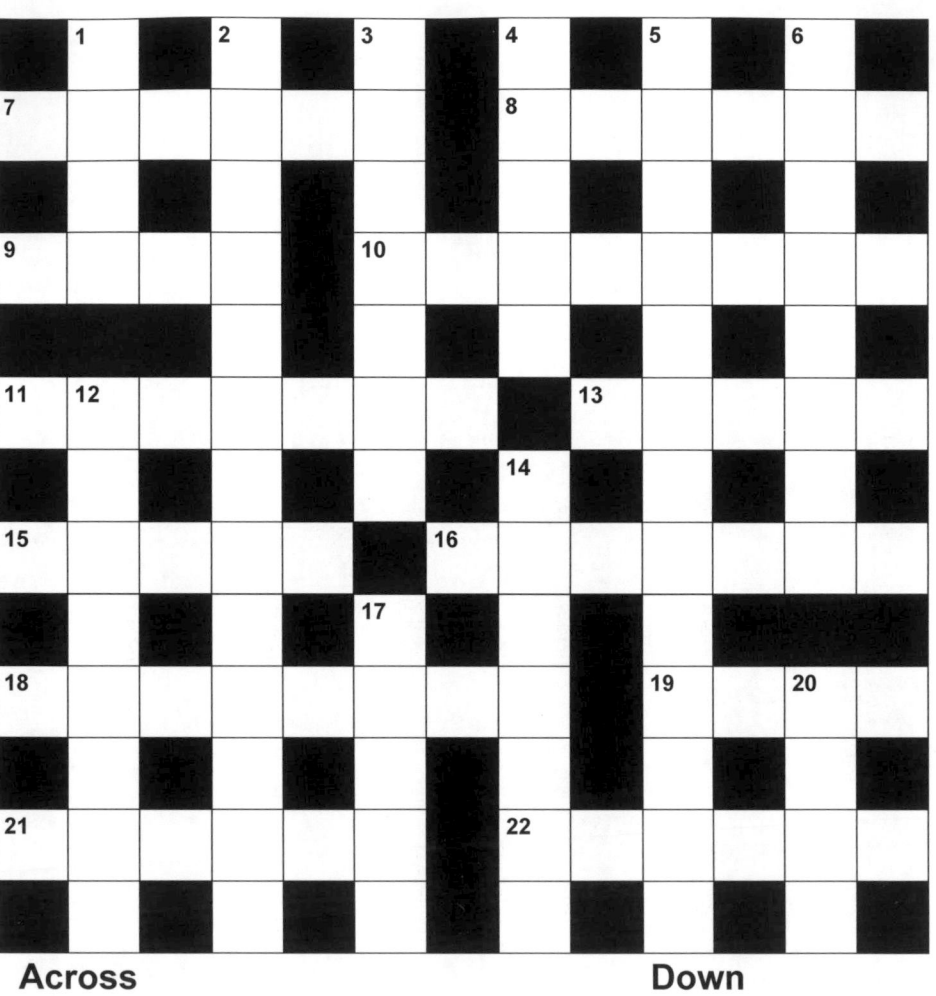

Across

7 - Fame (6)

8 - Large bodies of water (6)

9 - Skilful (4)

10 - Game of chance (8)

11 - Hottest (7)

13 - Perfume (5)

15 - Stomach (5)

16 - Driver of a horse-drawn vehicle (7)

18 - Salve (8)

19 - Rescue (4)

21 - Wonder at (6)

22 - City in NE Italy (6)

Down

1 - ___ Campbell: actress (4)

2 - Very thoughtful (13)

3 - Act of entering (7)

4 - Scoundrel (5)

5 - Railway and road intersection (5,8)

6 - Example (8)

12 - Native of the United States (8)

14 - Prisoner (7)

17 - Removes the skin from (5)

20 - Bad habit (4)

S	U	(T)	T	L	E		(E)	E	A	S	T	S
(A)		R		O		(E)		L		(R)		H
(P)	(D)	O	R	A	T	E		I		I		E
U		C		M		(O)	A	(R)	I	M	(Y)	L
I	T	(X)	H	Y		O		I				(F)
N		(B)				L	R	I	D	G	E	
		L		(M)	O	I	(W)	S		A		
(G)	A	I	R	E		T				T		R
E			S			I		(K)	L	A	C	E
R	I	S	O	(Z)	T	O		A		B		N
O		A		I		N	I	T	(V)	A	T	E
E		(Q)	N		S		H			S		(J)
S	(N)	E	(L)	(U)	H		U	S	(C)	E	R	(I)

A B C D E F G H I J K L M N O P Q R S T U V W X Y Z

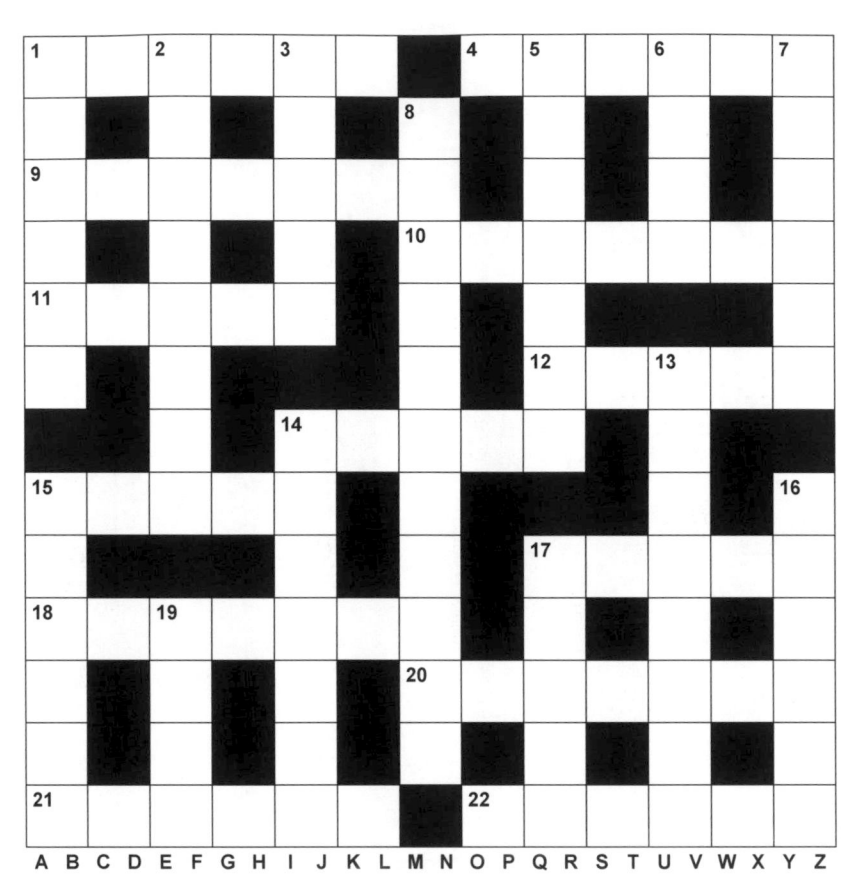

A B C D E F G H I J K L M N O P Q R S T U V W X Y Z

Across

1 - Harasses; hems in (6)

4 - Paler (6)

9 - Mythical bird (7)

10 - Turning forces (7)

11 - Dimensions (5)

12 - Young deer (5)

14 - Utilise (5)

15 - Strongly advised (5)

17 - Stringed instrument (5)

18 - Grotesque monster (7)

20 - Movement of vehicles (7)

21 - Oily (6)

22 - Mixed up or confused (6)

Down

1 - Go around (6)

2 - Dozing (8)

3 - Military vehicles (5)

5 - Distress greatly (7)

6 - Skirt worn by ballerinas (4)

7 - Lifts up (6)

8 - Estimate the value of (11)

13 - Unjustified (8)

14 - Sticks to (7)

15 - Free of an obstruction (6)

16 - Expressed vocally (6)

17 - Plait (5)

19 - Small piece of land (4)

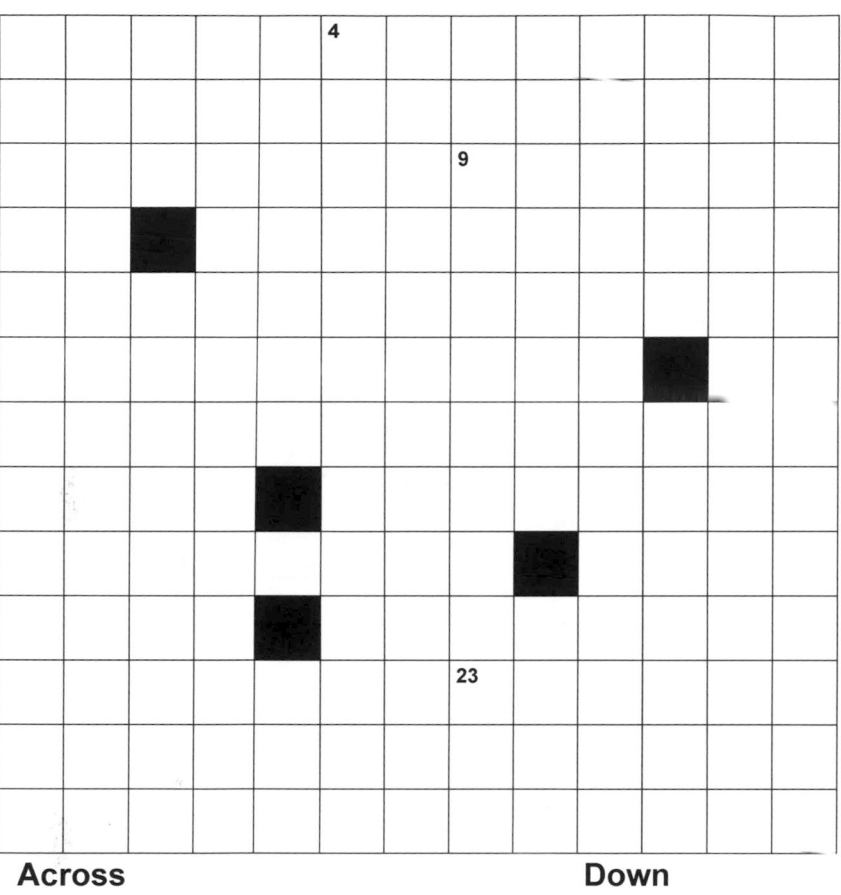

Across

1 - A lament

6 - Smile broadly

8 - Tropical bird

9 - Representation of a person

10 - Not well

11 - Leave out

12 - Make less sensitive

13 - Unfold

15 - Hanging down limply

17 - Make receptive or aware

20 - Bowed stringed instrument

21 - Muhammad ___ : boxing legend

22 - Small village

23 - Obligations

24 - Ruse

25 - Fragrant

Down

2 - Tribal leader

3 - Small heron

4 - Most favourable

5 - Give up

6 - Bison

7 - Standpoint

14 - Normally

15 - Definite; unquestionable

16 - Pointer (anag)

18 - Fishing net

19 - Consumer

20 - Essential

Across

1 - DSVWL

6 - FLK

8 - LMM

9 - NVY

10 - PLSM

12 - TSSL

13 - JSH

15 - LBBY

16 - RCT

17 - NDNGRS

Down

1 - DFNTLY

2 - VW

3 - WLDLY

4 - LMSTN

5 - PRCHTS

7 - DVSBL

11 - PLYD

14 - TRN

45

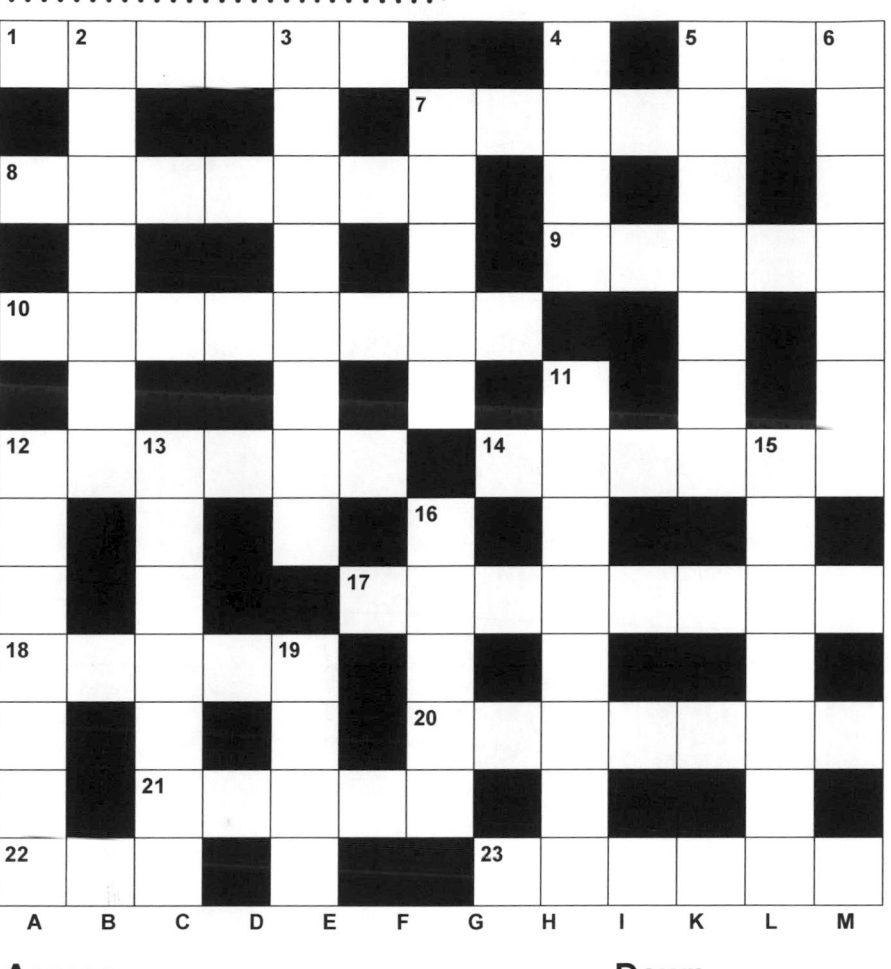

Across

1 - Drink (6)

5 - Performed an action (3)

7 - ___ Adkins: singer (5)

8 - Ascended (7)

9 - New ___ : Indian capital (5)

10 - Capable of being wrong (8)

12 - Positioned in the middle (6)

14 - Eg monkey or whale (6)

17 - Summon to return (4,4)

18 - Epic poem ascribed to Homer (5)

20 - Mercury alloy (7)

21 - Electronic message (5)

22 - Was in first place (3)

23 - Developed into (6)

Down

2 - Distance travelled (7)

3 - Relating to scripture (8)

4 - Fermented honey and water drink (4)

5 - Speak rhetorically (7)

6 - Anagram of 12 Down (7)

7 - Mix up (5)

11 - Eg rugby or tennis (4,4)

12 - Examination of one's health (7)

13 - Definite; unquestionable (7)

15 - Praise enthusiastically (7)

16 - Inner circle (5)

19 - Transaction (4)

Across

1 - Cook (4)

3 - Auction offers (4)

Down

1 - Suppress (4)

2 - Ventilates; supporters (4)

A B C D E F
H I N R S U

Across

3 - Lead singer of U2 (4)

4 - Dame (anag) (4)

5 - Where a bird lays eggs (4)

6 - A group of three (4)

7 - Killer whale (4)

Down

1 - Feeling of hatred (11)

2 - Not absolute (11)

51 Word Square

Short nail
Fit of shivering
Bend or coil
Brown seaweed

52 Word Square

Chair
Corner
Grows older
Critical examination

Across

7 - Give formal consent to (6)

8 - Bestow (6)

10 - Silklike fabric (7)

11 - Enlighten; educate morally (5)

12 - Ran away (4)

13 - Notable achievements (5)

17 - Concentrate on (5)

18 - At a distance (4)

22 - Hard rock (5)

23 - Rise into the air (of an aircraft) (4,3)

24 - Respite (6)

25 - Caress (6)

Down

1 - Please or delight (7)

2 - Manned (7)

3 - Later (5)

4 - Wooded areas (7)

5 - Attach (5)

6 - Becomes worn at the edges (5)

9 - Cautiously (9)

14 - Decade from 1940 to 1949 (7)

15 - Has enough money to pay for (7)

16 - Worked hard (7)

19 - Burning (5)

20 - Satiates (5)

21 - Currently in progress (5)

A B C D E F G H I J K L M N O P Q R S T U V W X Y Z

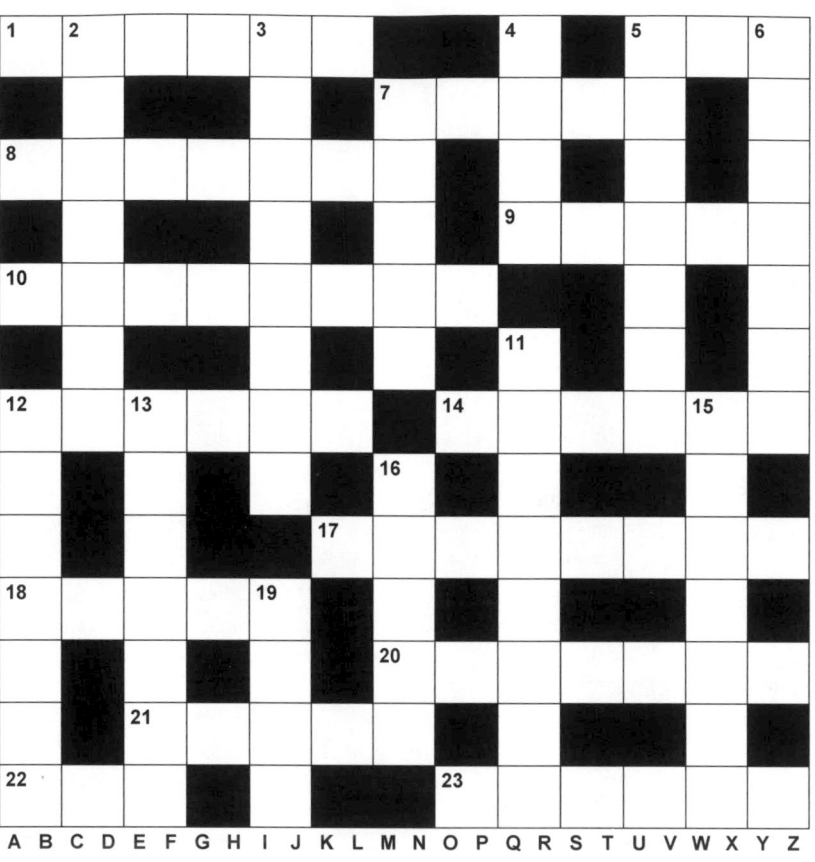

A B C D E F G H I J K L M N O P Q R S T U V W X Y Z

Across

1 - Undid (6)

5 - In what way (3)

7 - Stadium (5)

8 - Servile (7)

9 - U-shaped curve in a river (5)

10 - Misshapen (8)

12 - Adjusting a musical instrument (6)

14 - Jolted (6)

17 - Socially exclusive (8)

18 - Work out (5)

20 - Group of three plays (7)

21 - Baked sweet desserts (5)

22 - However (3)

23 - Believer in God (6)

Down

2 - Flat highland (7)

3 - Person leaving country (8)

4 - Nothing (4)

5 - Sheltered port (7)

6 - Disobedient (7)

7 - Concur (5)

11 - Conquer (8)

12 - Day of the week (7)

13 - Overlook (7)

15 - Flags of office (7)

16 - Narrow openings; lists (anag) (5)

19 - Northern deer (4)

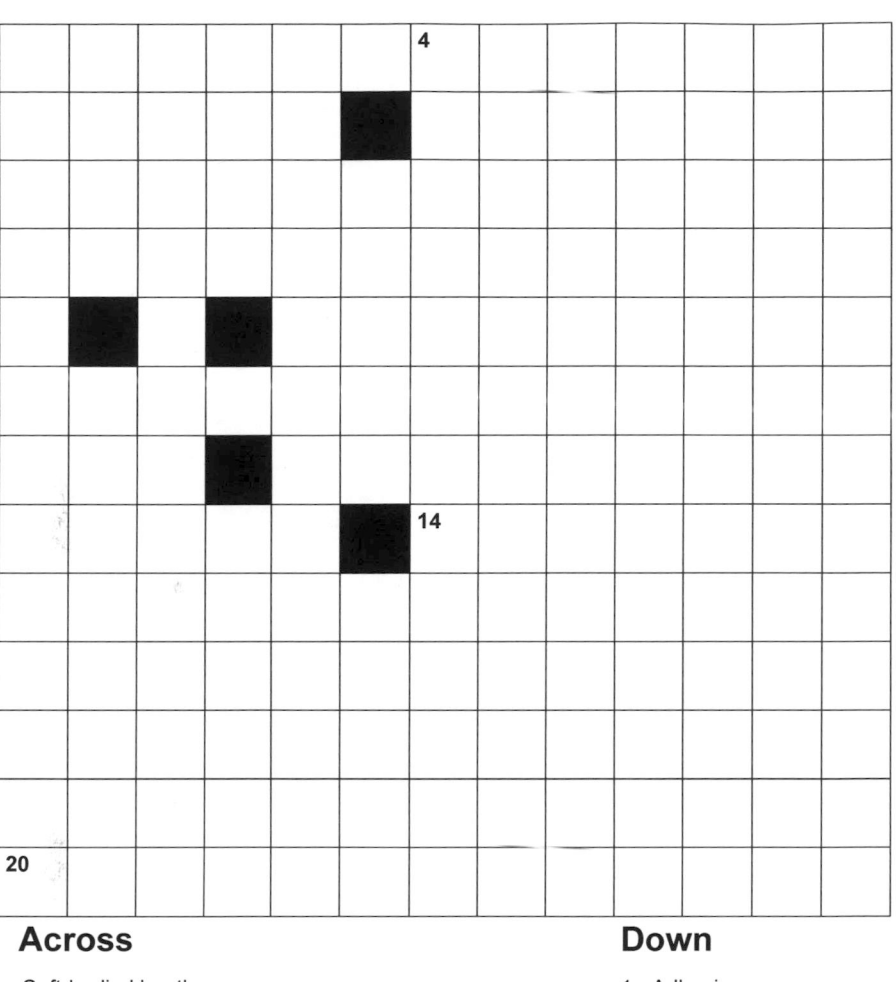

Across

1 - Soft-bodied beetle

5 - Fit of shivering

8 - Living in a city

9 - Caresses with the nose

10 - Alfresco

12 - Wishes for

14 - Wheeled supermarket vehicle

16 - Farm implements

18 - Perform in an exaggerated manner

19 - Opening of a cave

20 - Otherwise

21 - Piece of fabric that covers the head

Down

1 - Adhesive

2 - Paths of electrons around nuclei

3 - Conjecturing

4 - Donors (anag)

6 - Characteristically French

7 - Opposite of westerly

11 - Related to classification

12 - Show to be false

13 - Tools for drilling holes in rocks

14 - African fly

15 - Lapis ___ : blue gemstone

17 - Cook

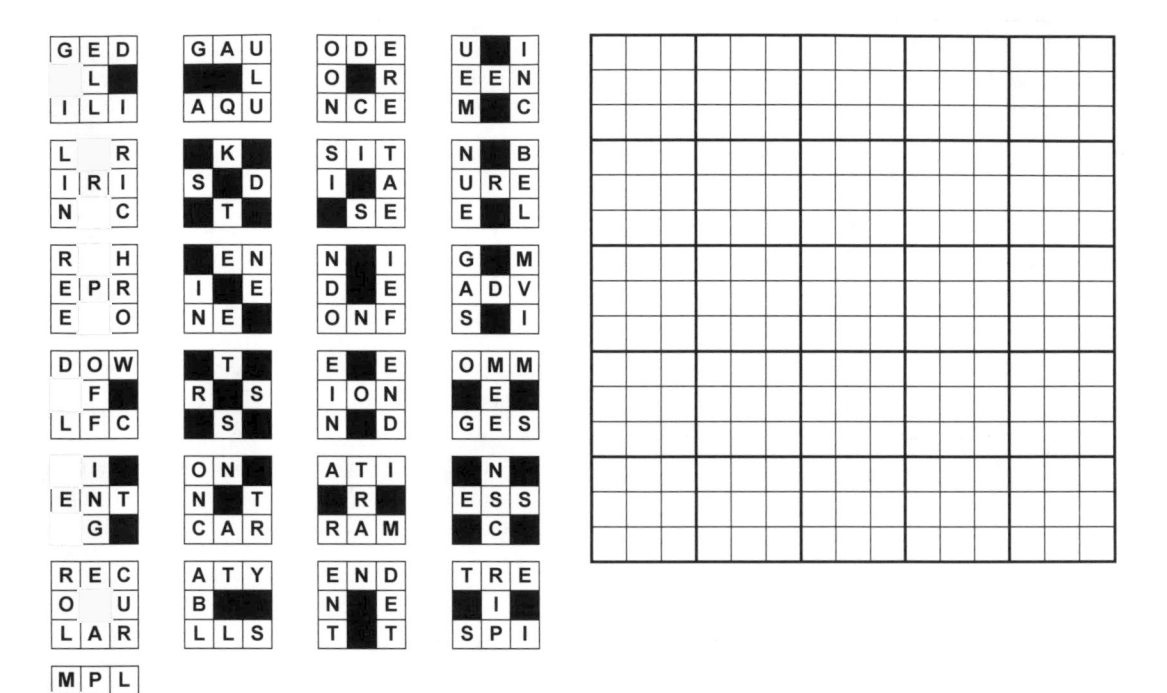

Can you slot the jigsaw pieces into the grid correctly, to create a completed crossword? Use the clues we have listed below to help you out. The grid exhibits standard crossword grid symmetry.

Across

1 - Favourable mention (14)

9 - Biggest (7)

10 - Passenger vehicle (7)

11 - Part of the eye (4)

12 - Severe recession (10)

14 - Estimated (6)

15 - Supplication (8)

17 - Like an eagle (8)

18 - Falls out unintentionally (6)

21 - Explorer (10)

22 - Observed (4)

24 - Take a seat (3,4)

25 - Collapse violently inwards (7)

26 - Belief in one's own ability (4-10)

Down

1 - Turning over and over (7)

2 - What CV stands for (10,5)

3 - Overly submissive (4)

4 - Course of a meal (6)

5 - Remove a monarch (8)

6 - Written copy (10)

7 - Extremely rarely (4,2,1,4,4)

8 - Up-to-date and fashionable (6)

13 - Reprimanding (7-3)

16 - Suggestive remark (8)

17 - Andre ___ : former US tennis player (6)

19 - Genuine (7)

20 - Trust or faith in (6)

23 - Potato (informal) (4)

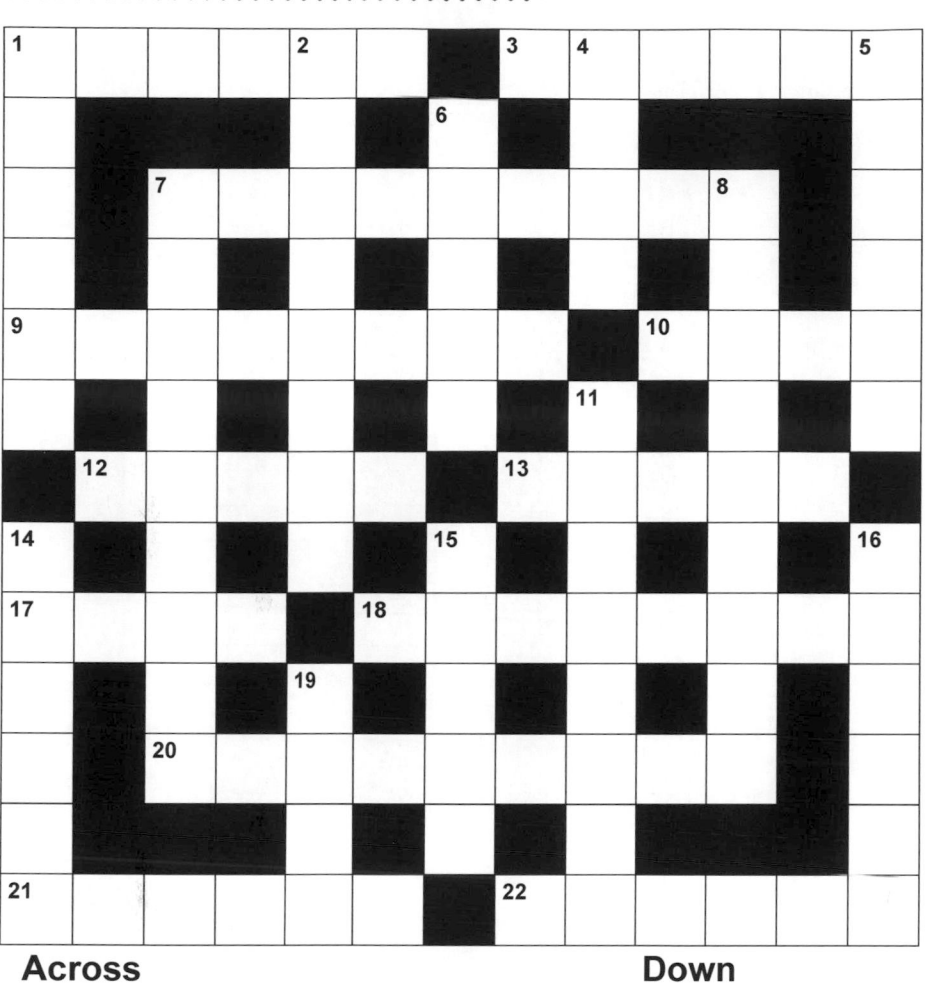

Across

1 - Grime or dirt (6)

3 - Concealing (6)

7 - Planning to do something (9)

9 - Occurred (8)

10 - Breathe convulsively (4)

12 - Sticks together (5)

13 - Established custom (5)

17 - Large wading bird (4)

18 - Person with a degree (8)

20 - Mexican dip (9)

21 - Waterproof overshoe (6)

22 - Mineral used to make plaster of Paris (6)

Down

1 - South American cowboy (6)

2 - Assembled (8)

4 - Egyptian goddess (4)

5 - Grouchy (6)

6 - Tines (anag) (5)

7 - Urging into action (9)

8 - Be attracted to a person or thing (9)

11 - Printed version of data on a computer (4,4)

14 - Employing (6)

15 - Big (5)

16 - Inert gaseous element (6)

19 - Head coverings (4)

Across

1 - EQIAMURANA

5 - DEPTI

7 - GHIET

9 - CYLLOD

10 - AGTS

12 - EIMT

13 - RCLIOF

16 - ORBTO

17 - IBDUA

18 - IMSMEPHEBR

Down

1 - ETCAZ

2 - SADLEM

3 - DURE

4 - CTBIHNGLU

6 - TLAALAPEB

8 - GTU

11 - RARETD

12 - AMR

14 - MICPH

15 - TBAS

60 Every Letter Counts

Across

1 - Accurate pieces of information (5)

3 - Prod with the elbow (5)

Down

1 - Scowl (5)

2 - Skewer; spear (5)

A C D E F G I K
N O P R S T U W

61 Ladder Crossword

Across

3 - Image of a god (4)

4 - Decapod crustacean (4)

5 - Pitcher (4)

6 - Uncle's wife (4)

7 - Italian acknowledgement (4)

Down

1 - Inconsistency (11)

2 - Act of explaining in detail (11)

Across

1 - Drink greedily (6)

5 - Atmospheric murk; obscure (3)

7 - Bird droppings used as fertiliser (5)

8 - Disturb (7)

9 - Grows weary (5)

10 - Mirth (8)

12 - Stitching (6)

14 - Thick wet mud (6)

17 - Ferdinand ____ : Portuguese navigator (8)

18 - Entrance barriers (5)

20 - Measure of how pressing something is (7)

21 - Period of darkness (5)

22 - Pop music performance (3)

23 - Take into the body (of food) (6)

Down

2 - Improve equipment (7)

3 - Hating (8)

4 - Stick with a hook (4)

5 - Searched for food (7)

6 - Tough animal tissue (7)

7 - Units of heredity (5)

11 - Substance causing a reaction (8)

12 - Method of presenting a play (7)

13 - Squandering (7)

15 - Sideways looks (7)

16 - The entire scale (5)

19 - Wise man (4)

57

R	○	A	N	D	A			○		I	○	Y
	A			○		B	O	○	E	R		E
○	R	U	I	S	E	R		Ł		I		A
	F		○		A		N	A	○	I	R	
○	○	N	D	A	N	○	O			I		N
	R		T		S		T		U			E
S	E	○	E	C	T		R	○	Y	M	E	D
Q		O		H		○		R			○	
○		G			V	E	○	O	○	O	U	S
A	M	○	E	R		A		T			E	
S		O		A		N	E	○	W	O	R	○
H		O	○	E	S		L			○		
○	A	K		E			D	○	L	A	Y	○

A B C D E F G H I J K L M N O P Q R S T U V W X Y Z

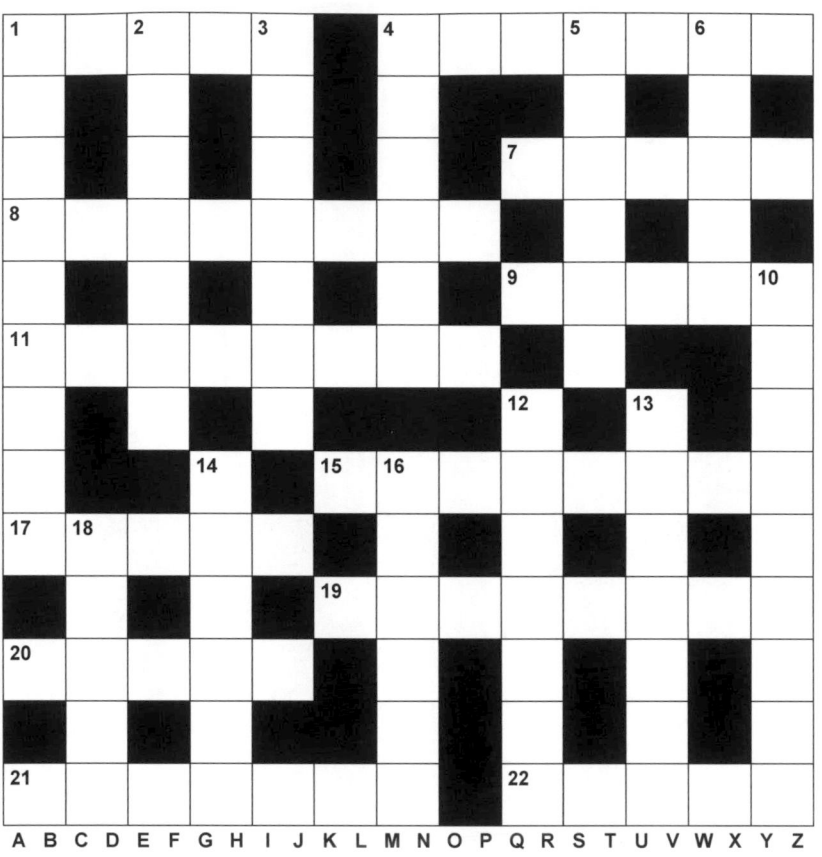

A B C D E F G H I J K L M N O P Q R S T U V W X Y Z

Across

1 - Shy (5)

4 - Temporary stay (7)

7 - Ire (5)

8 - Longevity of an individual (8)

9 - Supplant (5)

11 - Predominate (8)

15 - Being everywhere (8)

17 - Go stealthily or furtively (5)

19 - Umpires (8)

20 - Oven (5)

21 - Horrible (7)

22 - Besmirch (5)

Down

1 - Collections of implements (9)

2 - Anomalies (7)

3 - Flowers with white petals (7)

4 - Jumped up (6)

5 - Female giant (6)

6 - Part of generator (5)

10 - Synthetic fabric (9)

12 - Similar to water (7)

13 - Varied (7)

14 - Flow regulating devices (6)

16 - Windy (6)

18 - Indentation (5)

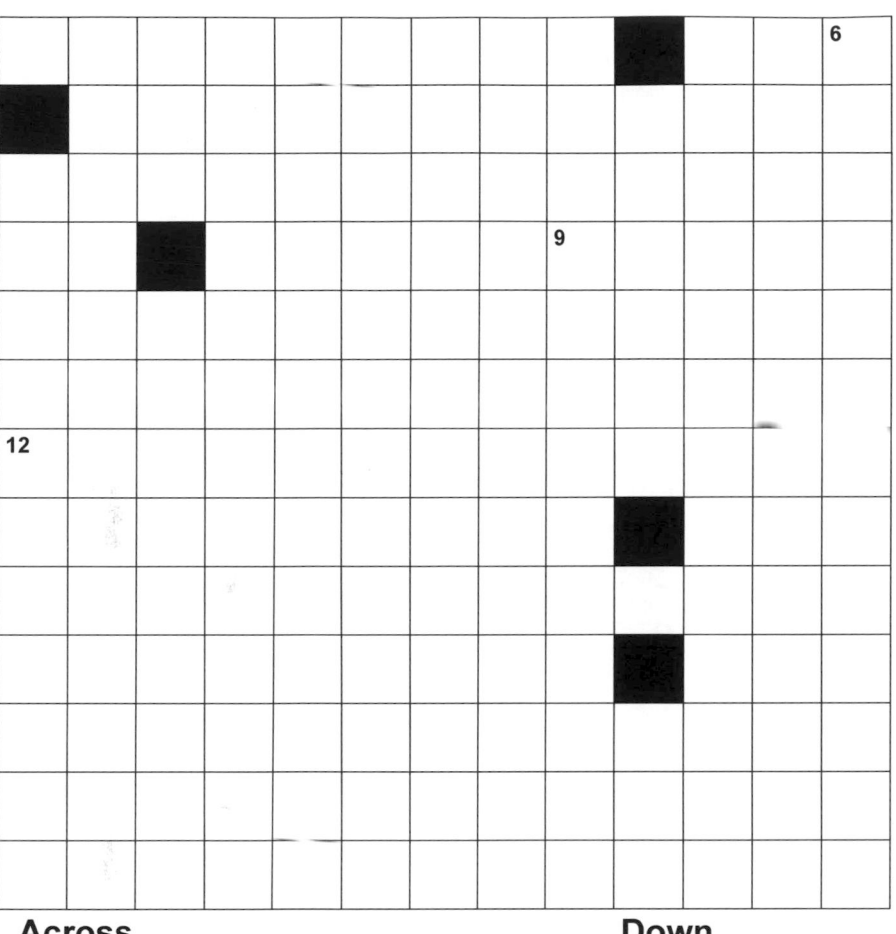

Across

1 - Repositories

5 - Cereal grain

7 - Leans at an angle

8 - Perceptible to the eye

9 - Crevices

10 - Distribute

12 - Stationary part of a motor

14 - Perceived

17 - Inhales

18 - ___ Robson: British tennis player

20 - Sheikdom in the Persian Gulf

21 - Not tight

22 - Saw (anag)

23 - Lethargic; sleepy

Down

2 - Snobbish

3 - Work surface

4 - Open tart

5 - Diffusion of molecules through a membrane

6 - Wrecked; binned

7 - Stretched tight (of a muscle)

11 - Figure of speech

12 - Swift-flying songbird

13 - Plants that live a year or less

15 - Foes

16 - Biter (anag)

19 - Long nerve fibre

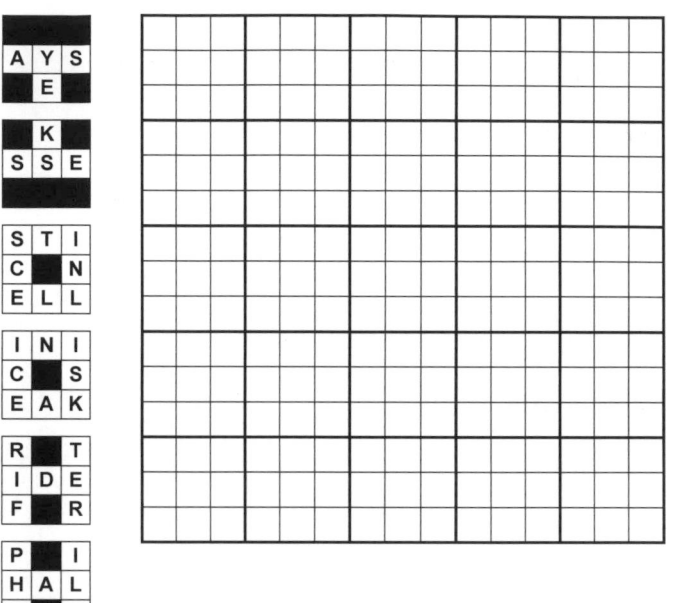

Can you slot the jigsaw pieces into the grid correctly, to create a completed crossword? Use the clues we have listed below to help you out. The grid exhibits standard crossword grid symmetry.

Across

1 - Bovine animals (6)

4 - Of many different kinds (8)

9 - Standard; usual (6)

10 - Evaluator (8)

11 - Long locks of hair (7)

13 - Final stage of a chess match (7)

14 - Defer action (13)

17 - Of mixed character (13)

20 - Large marine flatfish (7)

21 - Edge of a road (7)

23 - Garment worn after a shower (8)

24 - Type of sandwich (6)

25 - Considers in detail (8)

26 - Long thin line or band (6)

Down

1 - War memorial (8)

2 - Submarine weapon (7)

3 - Exposes secret information (5)

5 - Relation by marriage (6-2-3)

6 - In the red (9)

7 - Having a valid will (7)

8 - Moved very quickly (6)

12 - Vulnerable to (11)

15 - Fruit (9)

16 - Starlike symbol (8)

17 - Civilians trained as soldiers (7)

18 - Aperture or hole (7)

19 - Irrational fear (6)

22 - Microscopic fungus (5)

61

Across

7 - Spiny tree or shrub (6)

8 - Developed into (6)

10 - Extremely cold (7)

11 - Worthy principle or aim (5)

12 - Pleased (4)

13 - Hankered after (5)

17 - Third Greek letter (5)

18 - Every (4)

22 - Speak without preparation (2-3)

23 - Forbidden by law (7)

24 - Was deficient in (6)

25 - Assent or agree to (6)

Down

1 - Luggage (7)

2 - Broken stone used to surface roads (7)

3 - Impersonator (5)

4 - Unit of sound intensity (7)

5 - Name applied to something (5)

6 - Attractive young lady (5)

9 - Extortion by intimidation (9)

14 - Placed a bet (7)

15 - Wrangled over price (7)

16 - Cooled down (7)

19 - Long-handled spoon (5)

20 - Become suddenly understandable (5)

21 - Sudden jerk (5)

The last letter of each answer will become the first letter of the next answer.
Two other words will appear in the grey diagonals.

1 - Stubbornness
2 - Annuals
3 - Building examiner
4 - Saved from punishment
5 - Repudiates
6 - Residential areas
7 - Sat with legs wide apart
8 - ___ & Gabbana: fashion house
9 - Blows up
10 - Theatre worker
11 - Piece of furniture
12 - Repeat something once more
13 - Captive
14 - Official lists or records
15 - Pennant
16 - Take away
17 - Reduce one's expenditure
18 - Strange and mysterious
19 - Jellied ___ : English dish

69 Word Square

Domesticated pigs

US state

Female child

Marine flatfish

63

Drift in the air

Land measure

At liberty

Adolescent (abbrev)

71 Word Square

Labels

Spots

Bite at persistently

Stitches

Across

1 - Outdo (5)

3 - Is aware of (5)

Down

1 - Opposite of thin (5)

2 - Takes part in a game (5)

A C H I K L M N
O P R S T U W Y

Across

3 - Vases (4)

4 - Seal of the Archbishop of York (4)

5 - On top of (4)

6 - Move about aimlessly (4)

7 - US pop star (4)

Down

1 - System of government (11)

2 - Stargazers (11)

Across

1 - Flour and water mixture (5)

4 - Spiny egg-laying mammal (7)

7 - Earthy pigment (5)

8 - Careless (8)

9 - New ___ : Indian capital (5)

11 - Type of resistor (8)

15 - To come nearer to (8)

17 - Type of diagram (5)

19 - Mountainous region (8)

20 - Legendary stories (5)

21 - Warming devices (7)

22 - A person's leg (5)

Down

1 - Not acting decisively (9)

2 - Showed a person to their seat (7)

3 - Unfortunate (7)

4 - ___ Cuthbert: Kim Bauer in 24 (6)

5 - Units of linear measure (6)

6 - Compass point (5)

10 - Not in possession of the facts (2,3,4)

12 - Sharp no (anag) (7)

13 - ___ Bedingfield: musician (7)

14 - Eventual outcome (6)

16 - Little bottles (6)

18 - Type of verse (5)

R	E	M	I	○	■	○	U	A	C	○	E	D
E	■	I	■	○	■	U	■	■	O	■	R	■
V	■	S	■	A	■	E	■	E	N	○	○	R	Y
○	○	L	A	○	○	U	■	○	■	D	■
L	■	A	■	I	■	E	■	B	E	Z	E	L
S	L	I	○	N	E	○	S	■	○	■	I
I	■	D	■	○	■	■	B	■	○	■	F
O	■	S	■	○	G	G	R	○	E	V	E
N	I	○	C	E	■	H	E	R	■	○
■	R	■	A	■	P	O	W	E	R	F	U	L
B	O	I	L	S	■	S	○	E	■	O
■	N	■	A	■	T	E	C	O
○	○	P	○	E	S	S	■	D	O	T	E	○

A B C D E F G H I J K L M N O P Q R S T U V W X Y Z

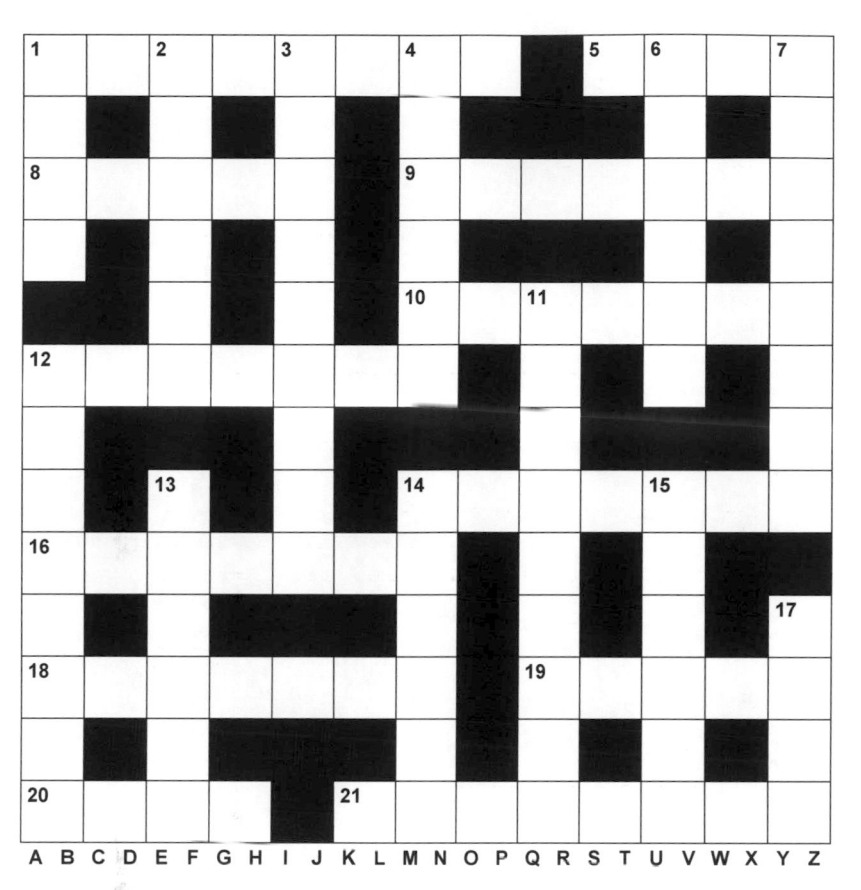

A B C D E F G H I J K L M N O P Q R S T U V W X Y Z

Across

1 - Compartment of a train (8)

5 - Requests (4)

8 - Covered with water (5)

9 - Water bearing rock (7)

10 - Dispossess (7)

12 - Science of matter and energy (7)

14 - Biological catalysts (7)

16 - Domain (7)

18 - Playhouse (7)

19 - Dreadful (5)

20 - Government tax (4)

21 - Amazes (8)

Down

1 - Cover (4)

2 - Actually (6)

3 - Gained through heredity (9)

4 - Organs (6)

6 - Element added to the end of a word (6)

7 - Snakes (8)

11 - Way of plucking violin strings (9)

12 - Put in a pouch (8)

13 - Add (6)

14 - Remains of fire (6)

15 - Small cake-like bread (6)

17 - Expression of regret (4)

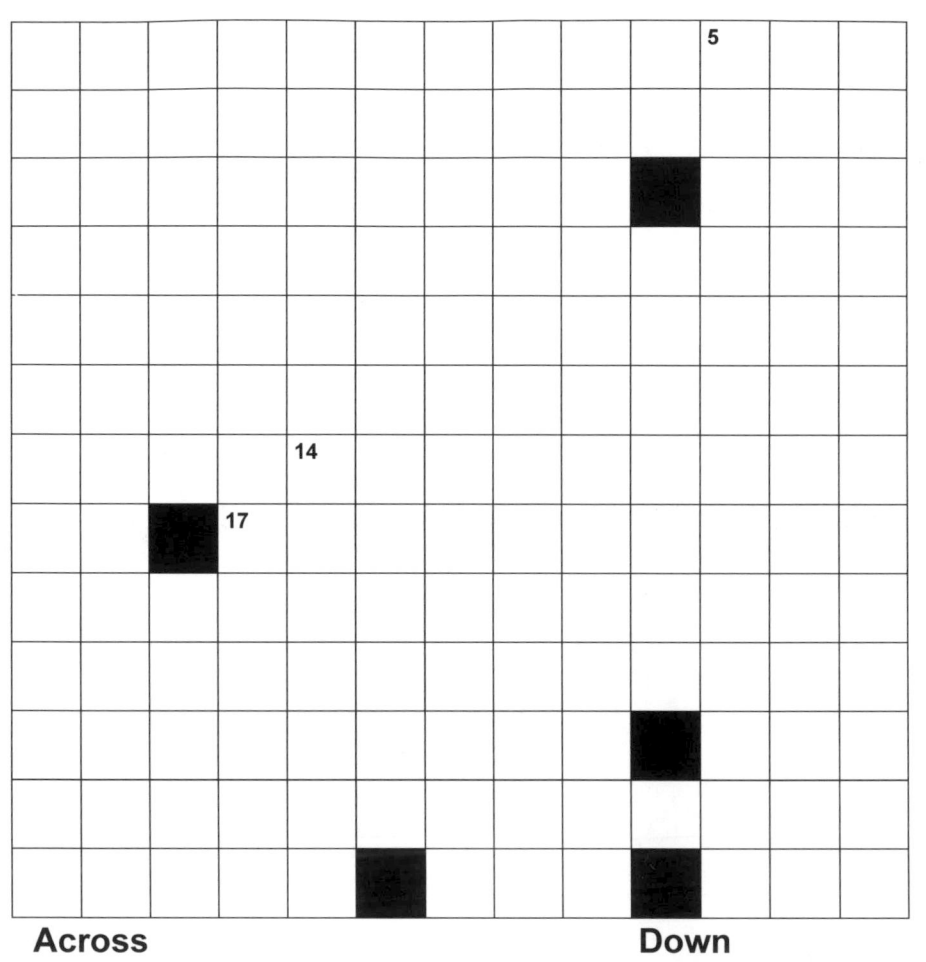

Across

7 - Contemptibly small

8 - Hanging down limply

10 - Ban on publication

11 - Short musical composition

12 - Give up one's rights

13 - Simple

17 - A poison

18 - Outdoor swimming pool

22 - Praise enthusiastically

23 - Hero of the Odyssey

24 - Plant spikes

25 - Lays eggs

Down

1 - Call the validity of a practice into question

2 - Brazilian dance

3 - ___ Balding: TV presenter

4 - Poisonous metallic element

5 - Position or point

6 - Woody tissue

9 - Insatiable

14 - Type of knot

15 - Puzzles composed of many pieces

16 - Be composed of

19 - Tends (anag)

20 - Device for sharpening razors

21 - Slender woman or girl

78 Vowelless Crossword

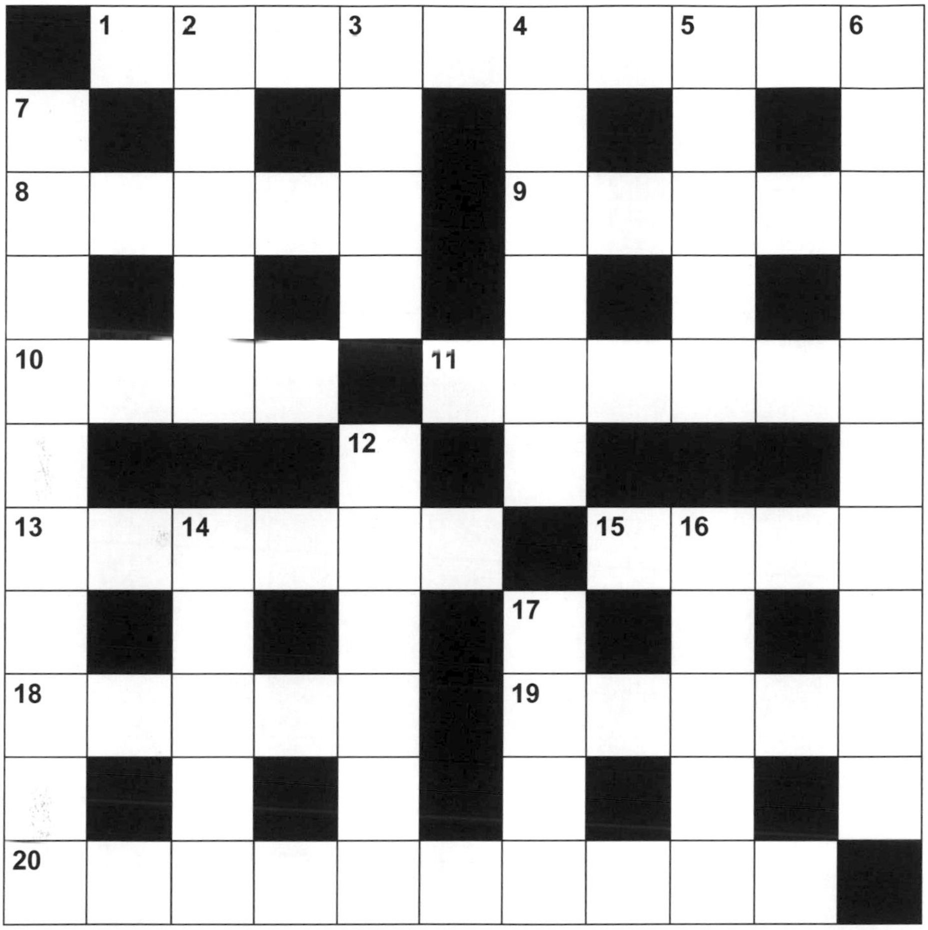

Across

1 - SSRTMNT

8 - DLR

9 - D

10 - CN

11 - NTN

13 - NST

15 - THM

18 - NRT

19 - RMN

20 - XPLNNG

Down

2 - SLV

3 - GR

4 - TRCS

5 - DCT

6 - TRNMNT

7 - DMNTV

12 - MNTR

14 - SHP

16 - HMN

17 - WRN

Across

7 - Standard; usual (6)

8 - Capital of Canada (6)

10 - Aromatic herb (7)

11 - Small antelope (5)

12 - Require (4)

13 - Academy award (5)

17 - Prod with the elbow (5)

18 - Where darts players throw from (4)

22 - Spring flower (5)

23 - Exceeds; surpasses (7)

24 - Beginner (6)

25 - Extraterrestrial rock (6)

Down

1 - Continuing (7)

2 - Commanded (7)

3 - Maritime (5)

4 - Piece of furniture (7)

5 - Frenzied (5)

6 - Conjuring trick (5)

9 - Roman Catholic prelate (9)

14 - Go faster than (7)

15 - Tenth month of the year (7)

16 - Ascertain dimensions (7)

19 - Natural satellites (5)

20 - Small fruit used for oil (5)

21 - Semiaquatic mammal (5)

Across

7 - EGELI

8 - MOSEO

9 - RTUORIB

10 - EAS

11 - SRVIINCTEDE

14 - LAE

16 - AMILCCU

19 - LREAY

20 - EKELS

Down

1 - BBOL

2 - RRENEA

3 - EIMS

4 - BSEMSO

5 - GOSF

6 - TEDPRA

11 - LDEVUA

12 - ACDYSE

13 - XIEDET

15 - YAWR

17 - KALE

18 - TSAM

Across

1 - Big cat (5)

3 - Exhales air (5)

Down

1 - Pollex (5)

2 - Positions in a hierarchy (5)

A B E G H I K L
M N O R S T U W

82 Ladder Crossword

Across

3 - Travel at speed (4)

4 - Metal fastener (4)

5 - What we hear with (4)

6 - ___ Macpherson: supermodel (4)

7 - Highest adult male singing voice (4)

Down

1 - Award for third place (6,5)

2 - Type of fat (11)

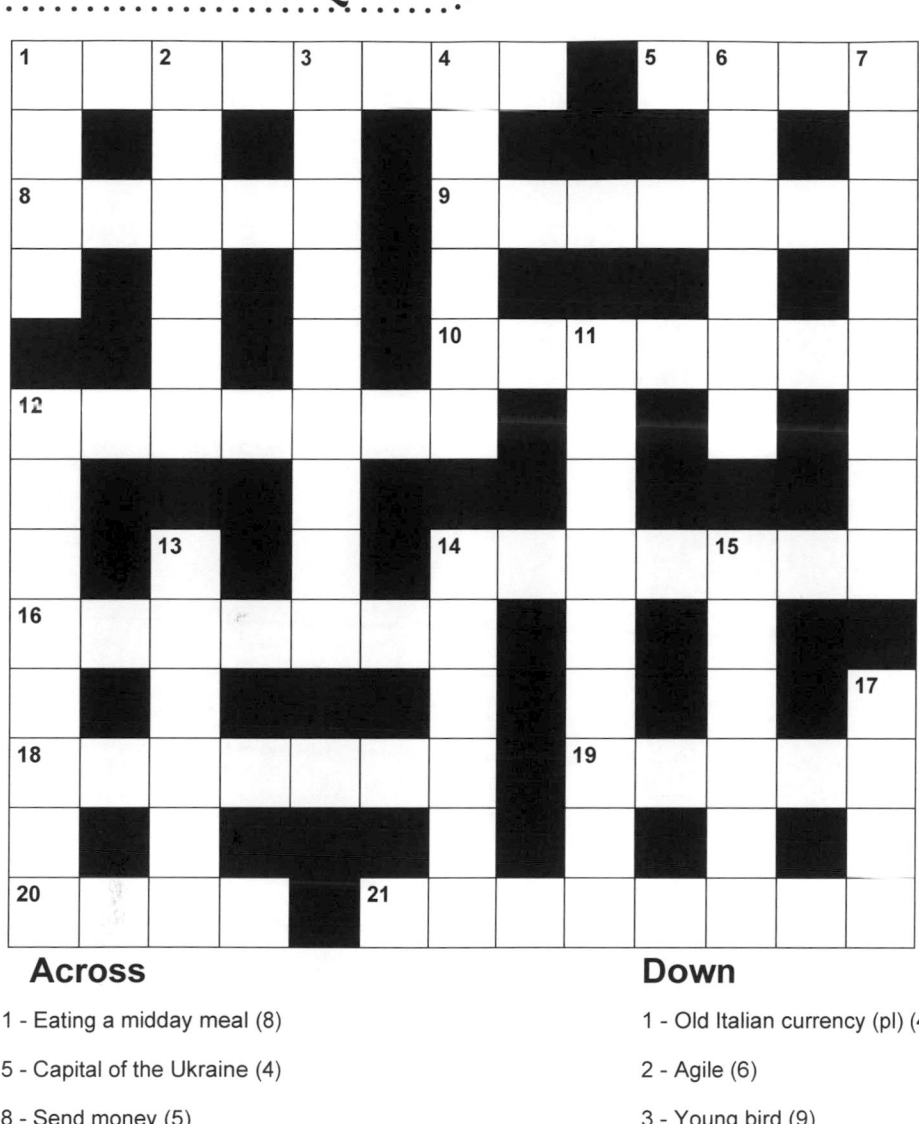

Across

1 - Eating a midday meal (8)

5 - Capital of the Ukraine (4)

8 - Send money (5)

9 - Pin tops (anag) (7)

10 - Compels to do something (7)

12 - Imaginary mischievous sprite (7)

14 - Cut pieces off something hard (7)

16 - Part of a gun (7)

18 - Car motors (7)

19 - Excuse of any kind (5)

20 - Abominable snowman (4)

21 - Getting away from (8)

Down

1 - Old Italian currency (pl) (4)

2 - Agile (6)

3 - Young bird (9)

4 - Concept (6)

6 - Cast doubt upon (6)

7 - Disappeared (8)

11 - US state (9)

12 - Shiny; sparkly (8)

13 - Move about restlessly (6)

14 - Serious situation (6)

15 - Type of sandwich (6)

17 - Chinese dynasty (4)

B	O	N	○	I	○	E	S	■	J	○	D	E
U	■	A	■	N	■	○	■	■	○	■	■	Y
M	I	M	I	C	■	○	○	I	D	I	○	E
○	■	E	■	U	■	L	■	■	○	■	B	
	■	L	■	○	■	V	O	U	C	H	R	
P	A	○	A	○	L	E	■	N	■	T	○	O
E	■	■	E	■	■	■	○	T	■	■	○	
R	■	E	■	○	■	○	U	I	C	○	E	S
○	○	J	○	○	S	U	■	P	■	I	■	
U	■	E	■	■	A	■	P	■	K	■	I	
R	A	○	C	O	O	N	■	I	○	E	A	S
E	■	T	■	■	T	■	N	■	R	■	L	
R	I	S	○	■	L	A	R	G	E	S	S	E

A B C D E F G H I J K L M N O P Q R S T U V W X Y Z

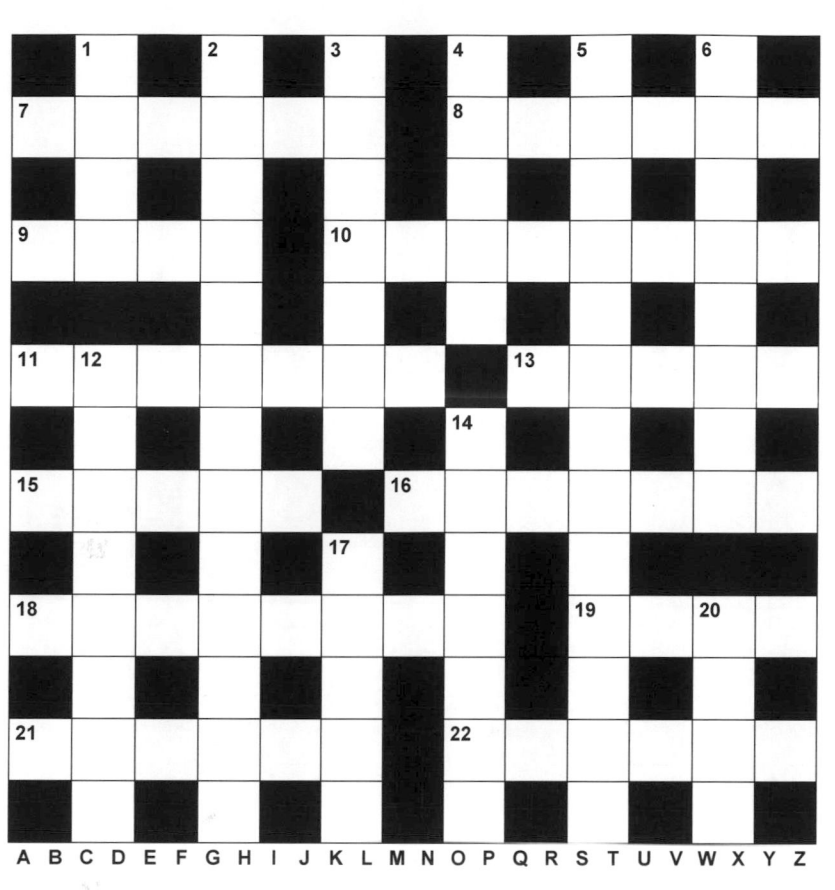

A B C D E F G H I J K L M N O P Q R S T U V W X Y Z

Across

7 - Type of sausage (6)

8 - Tiny fish (6)

9 - Article of clothing (4)

10 - Discern (8)

11 - Overturned (7)

13 - Sea inlet (5)

15 - Healthy skin transplanted (5)

16 - Made the sound of a duck (7)

18 - Bodily exertion (8)

19 - Linear unit (4)

21 - Advance evidence for (6)

22 - First weekday (6)

Down

1 - Father (4)

2 - The fifth period of the Palaeozoic era (13)

3 - Skin eruptions (7)

4 - Shadow (5)

5 - Exclamations such as 'dear me!' (13)

6 - Come together (8)

12 - Bleach (8)

14 - Repositories of antiques (7)

17 - Measured or classified (5)

20 - Converse (4)

Across

1 - Tennis officials

4 - Light canoe

7 - Motet (anag)

8 - Make less taut

9 - Monetary unit of South Africa

10 - Material from which metal is extracted

11 - Sued (anag)

15 - Sailor of a light vessel

17 - Invalid; void

19 - That vessel

20 - Finish

24 - Give authority to

25 - Hazardous; dangerous

26 - Extinct birds

27 - Contrast

Down

1 - Complete; absolute

2 - Power; strength

3 - Inclined plane

4 - ___ Egan: Westlife singer

5 - Bonds of union

6 - Royal domain

8 - Framework for moving the injured

12 - Very cold

13 - ___ Winehouse: singer

14 - Compete

16 - ___ Bedingfield: musician

18 - Oily organic compound

21 - Recipient of money

22 - Nocturnal birds of prey

23 - Small drink of spirits

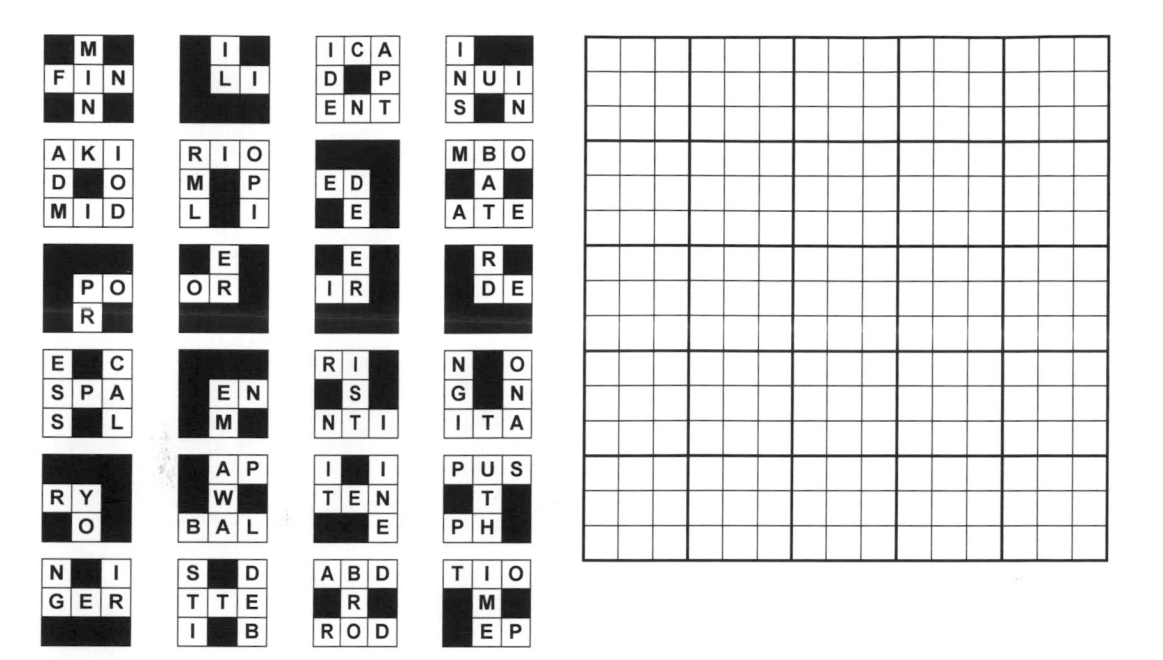

Can you slot the jigsaw pieces into the grid correctly, to create a completed crossword? Use the clues we have listed below to help you out. The grid exhibits standard crossword grid symmetry.

Across

4 - Dissatisfaction; boredom (5)

6 - Items made from fired clay (7)

8 - Failure to fulfil a duty (10)

9 - Musical composition (4)

10 - Gnawing animal like a rat (6)

11 - Statement of commemoration (7)

12 - Given to thievery (5-8)

16 - Relating to knowledge based on deduction (1,6)

17 - With hands on the hips (6)

19 - Spherical object (4)

20 - Overawe (10)

21 - Feeling of hopelessness (7)

22 - Singing voice (5)

Down

1 - Within a space (6)

2 - Hurting; throbbing (8)

3 - Suave; stylish (8)

4 - Involve in conflict (7)

5 - Paint (anag) (5)

6 - Head of the government (5,8)

7 - Period between childhood and adulthood (5)

13 - Lacking intelligence and sense (8)

14 - Hot and humid (8)

15 - Arguer (7)

16 - Prize (5)

17 - Confess to be true (5)

18 - One of the halogens (6)

Across

7 - ___ Keys: US singer (6)

8 - Modern ballroom dance (3-3)

9 - Put down (4)

10 - Electronic message (5)

12 - Ascend (5)

14 - Every (4)

16 - Opposite of low (4)

18 - Camel-like animal (5)

20 - Assumed proposition (5)

22 - Throb; dull pain (4)

25 - Cut down a tree (6)

26 - ___ Wood: US actor (6)

Down

1 - Simple non-flowering plant (4)

2 - Sour to the taste (6)

3 - Water barrier (3)

4 - Highest point (4)

5 - Front of a building (6)

6 - Cup (7)

11 - Clock face (4)

13 - Smile broadly (4)

15 - Dealt with a tough question (7)

17 - Mark ___ : US actor (6)

19 - Spiny tree or shrub (6)

21 - Helper; assistant (4)

23 - Become healthy again (of a wound) (4)

24 - Nourished (3)

89 Every Letter Counts

Across

1 - Smash (5)

3 - Rounded protuberances on camels (5)

Down

1 - Bungle (5)

2 - Furnaces (5)

A B C E H I K L
M N O P R S T U

90 Ladder Crossword

Across

3 - Rime (anag) (4)

4 - Long periods of history (4)

5 - High fidelity (abbrev) (2-2)

6 - Simple non-flowering plant (4)

7 - British nobleman (4)

Down

1 - Calm and sensible (5-6)

2 - Radically (11)

Across

7 - EHTME

8 - AUCIR

9 - CAUIBVO

10 - IBN

11 - BTNOCOINUAR

14 - BNA

16 - OCSNREF

19 - UINRE

20 - ITRAL

Down

1 - BAST

2 - ENAEVL

3 - UEPR

4 - CAIACA

5 - BCIR

6 - NINNAT

11 - CDIAND

12 - IRCHSE

13 - BAIERI

15 - BLRU

17 - STNE

18 - OSLE

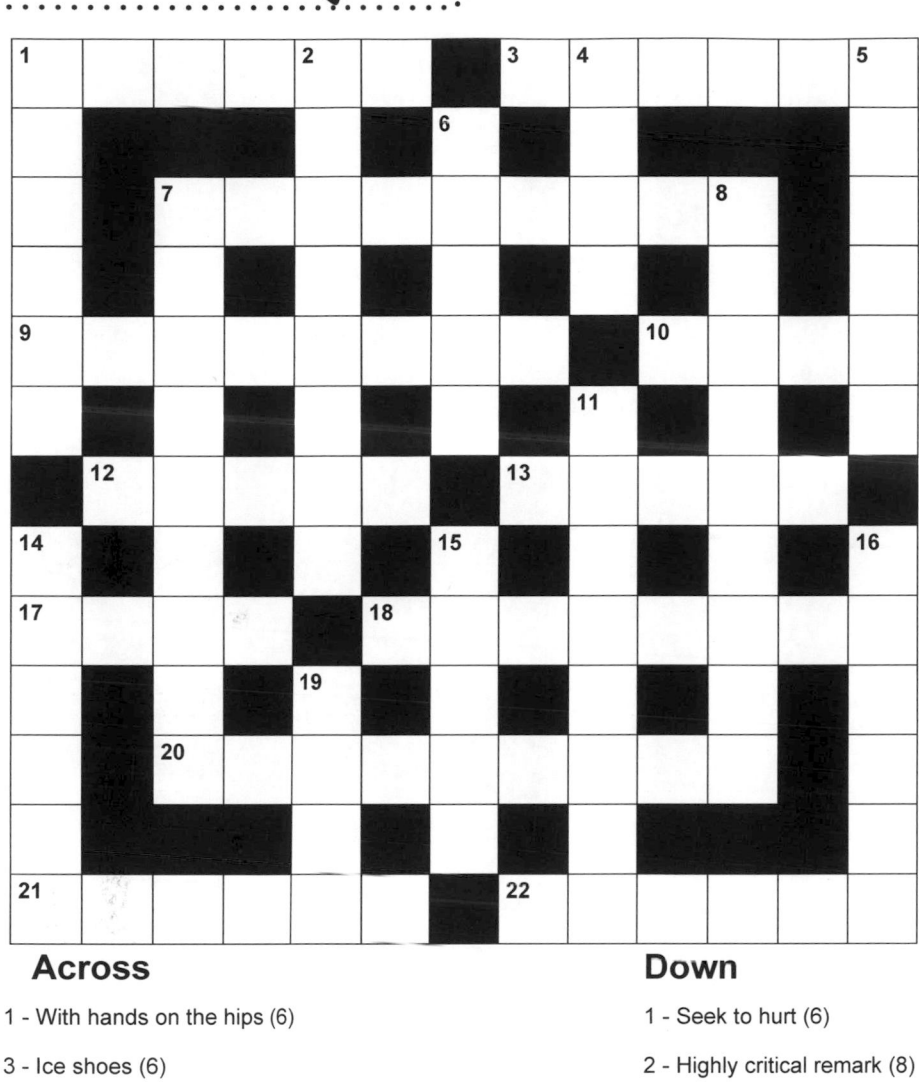

Across

1 - With hands on the hips (6)

3 - Ice shoes (6)

7 - Chunkiness (9)

9 - Excellent (8)

10 - Garment for the foot (4)

12 - Skewered meat (5)

13 - Drenches (5)

17 - ___ Egan: Westlife singer (4)

18 - Small pocket tool (8)

20 - General erudition (9)

21 - Eg Athenians (6)

22 - Uttered (6)

Down

1 - Seek to hurt (6)

2 - Highly critical remark (8)

4 - Capital of the Ukraine (4)

5 - Long-legged wading birds (6)

6 - Sinks (anag) (5)

7 - Officially registered name (9)

8 - Accumulate for future use (9)

11 - Excessively emotional (6,2)

14 - Popular winter sport (6)

15 - Flat-bottomed vessels (5)

16 - Establish by calculation (6)

19 - Snatched (4)

					S		U	U		U			
D		B	U				P		N	A		A	
	T		R	E	S		S			A			
	A		I		O	E			L	L	Y		
	S			E		T		E		L			
T		A	D	E	R	S		O	S	I	E	R	
	E		I		S			T		S			
A	B	A	C	K		A	R	I	A	T	E		
	U		T		S		O						
E	T			O	P	I	A		N	O		E	
	T			A				I		U			
R	A	I	N	E	D		L	U	N	A		Y	
			S		S	E	E		E		T		

A B C D E F G H I J K L M N O P Q R S T U V W X Y Z

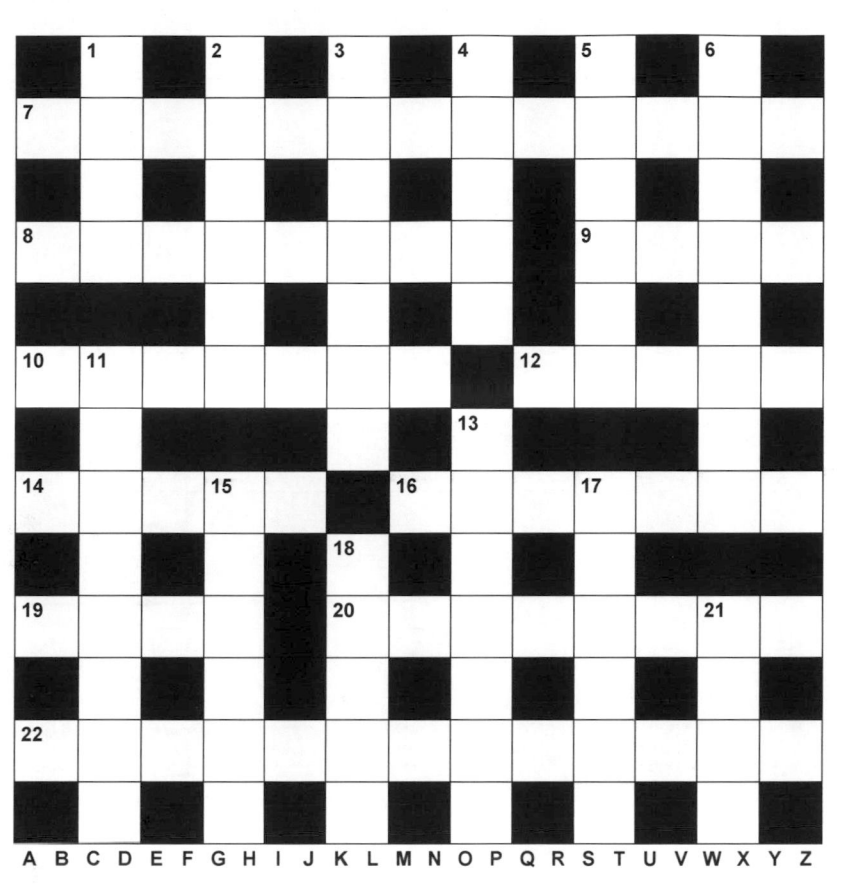

Across

7 - In an absorbing manner (13)

8 - Dependable (8)

9 - Ask questions (4)

10 - Imprisonment (7)

12 - Accolade (5)

14 - Puff on cigarette (5)

16 - Male sibling (7)

19 - Affirm solemnly (4)

20 - Thawed (8)

22 - Lacking complexity (13)

Down

1 - Sheet of paper (4)

2 - Metamorphic rock (6)

3 - Anyone (7)

4 - Spirited horse (5)

5 - Incomparable (6)

6 - Last (8)

11 - Motionless (8)

13 - Movement of vehicles (7)

15 - Show servile deference (6)

17 - Chest (6)

18 - Leaps (5)

21 - Not odd (4)

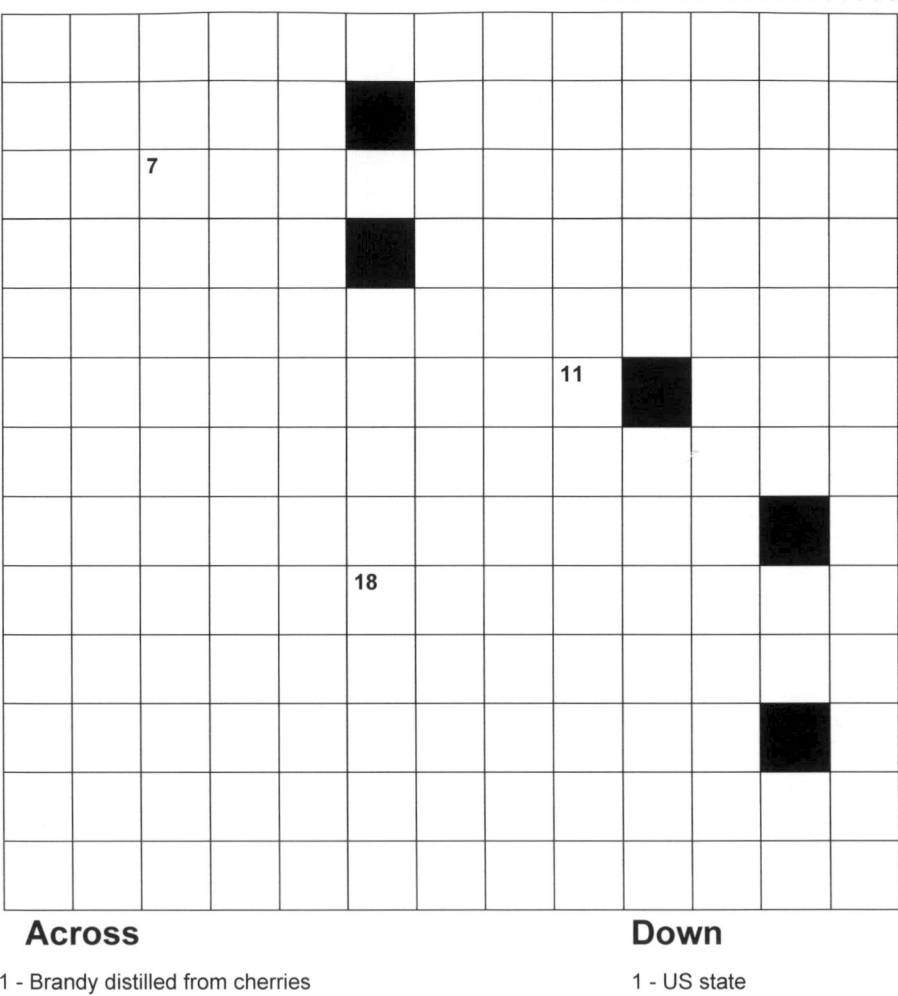

Across

1 - Brandy distilled from cherries

3 - Feeling a continuous dull pain

7 - Halted temporarily

9 - Food of the gods

10 - ___ of Wight: largest island of England

12 - Tool for boring holes

13 - Skewered meat

17 - Not at home

18 - Curved surface of a liquid in a tube

20 - Opposite of lateness

21 - Vitreous

22 - Thoroughfare

Down

1 - US state

2 - Person who buys goods

4 - Give up one's rights

5 - Classifies; sorts

6 - Send money

7 - Conquer; master

8 - Moves away from

11 - Army unit

14 - Seizing

15 - Darken

16 - Feature

19 - Part of the eye

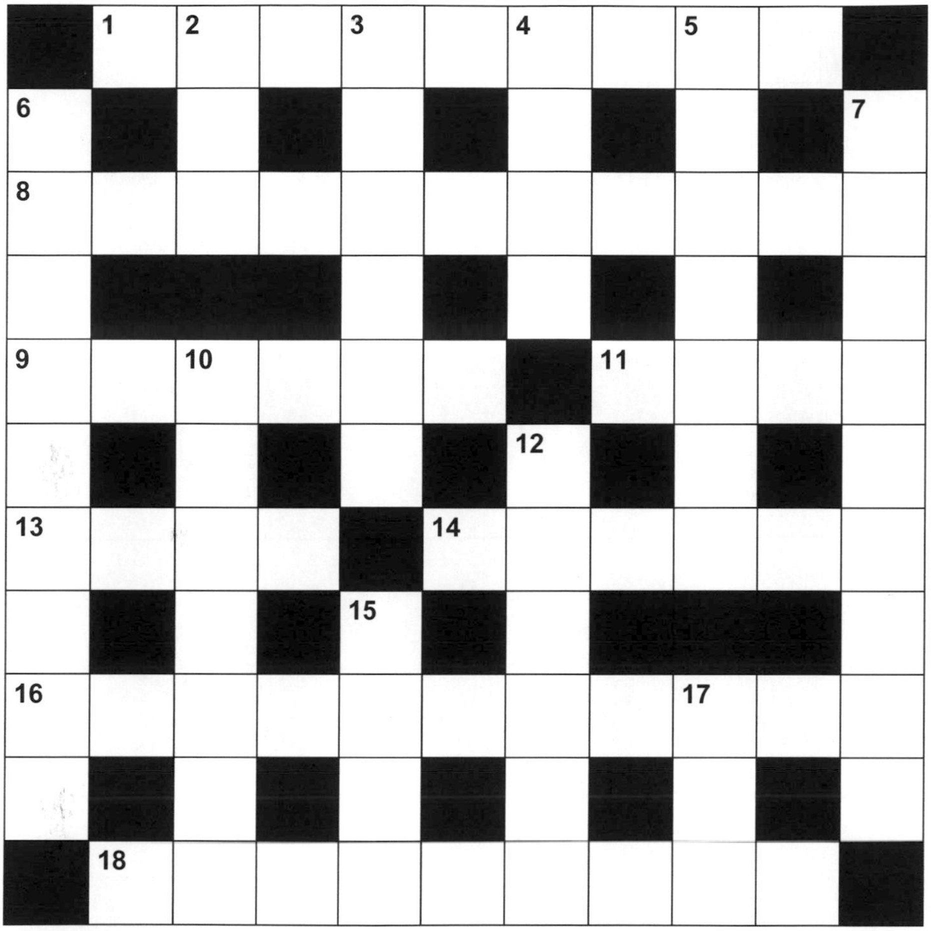

Across

1 - BNDND

8 - BSRVTRY

9 - SCLR

11 - VS

13 - RL

14 - WLNT

16 - CMPSTN

18 - BLLK

Down

2 - BS

3 - NRML

4 - VL

5 - MTN

6 - HPSCTCH

7 - BYZNTN

10 - NM

12 - LMN

15 - YG

17 - NK

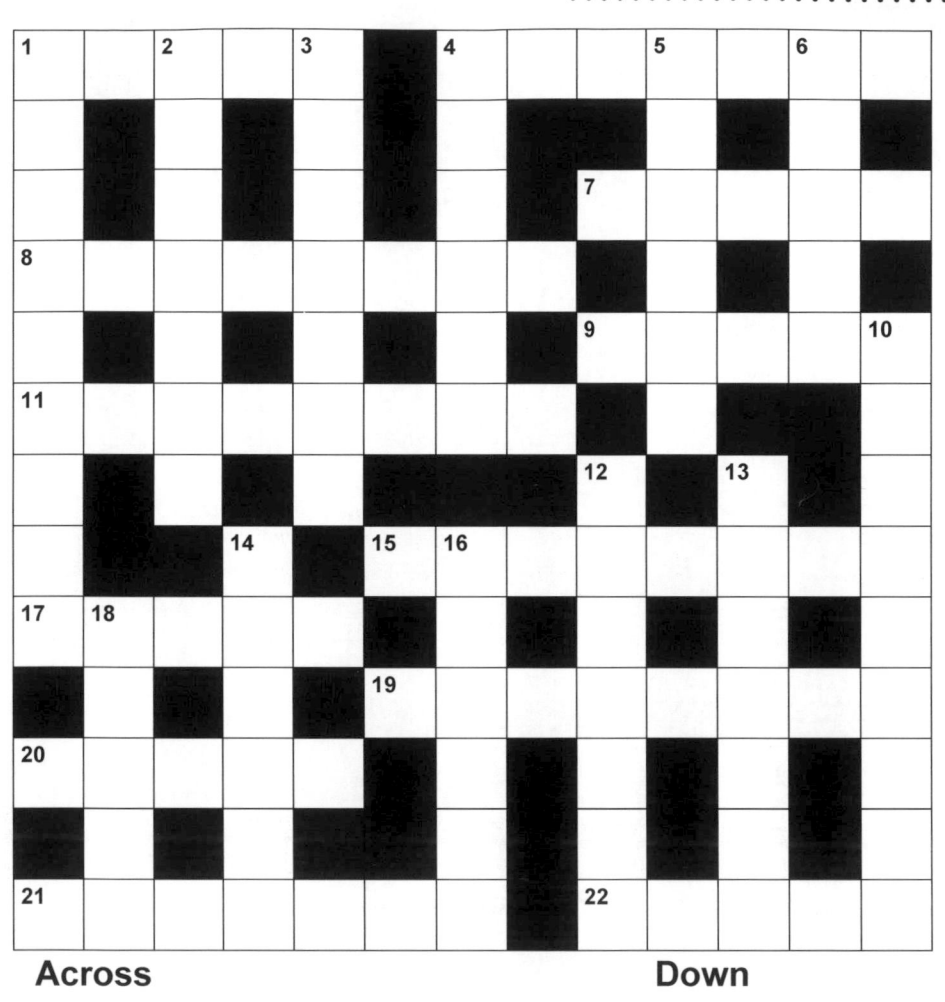

Across

1 - Rises (anag) (5)

4 - Having a valid will (7)

7 - Bad-tempered (5)

8 - Private detective (8)

9 - Item of clothing (5)

11 - Showing deep and solemn respect (8)

15 - Large fish (8)

17 - Journeys (5)

19 - Breaking in two (8)

20 - Breathe out loudly when asleep (5)

21 - Chooses (7)

22 - Levies (5)

Down

1 - Written below the line (of text) (9)

2 - Keep for future use (7)

3 - Seafarers (7)

4 - Bird with a long coloured beak (6)

5 - Main tree stems (6)

6 - Relit (anag) (5)

10 - Adolescents (9)

12 - Set of three things (7)

13 - Musical performance (7)

14 - Not dense (6)

16 - Sport Andy Murray plays (6)

18 - Wash with clean water (5)

98 Every Letter Counts

Across

1 - Remove errors from software (5)

3 - Opposite of tall (5)

Down

1 - Curbs (5)

2 - Gleam; glitter (5)

A B D E G H I L
M N O P R S T U

99 Ladder Crossword

Across

3 - Hoodwink (4)

4 - Domesticated (of animals) (4)

5 - Pleased (4)

6 - Long nerve fibre (4)

7 - Frozen rain (4)

Down

1 - The recording of a still image (11)

2 - Extremely (11)

Frozen rain

Breezy

Type of golf club

Medium-sized feline

1

I	N	D	I	A		G	R	A	N	D	E	E
M		E		T		A		A		L		
P		A		T		U		S	T	R	A	Y
A	U	D	I	E	N	C	E		U		T	
R		P		N		H		A	R	M	E	D
T	E	A	R	D	R	O	P		E			E
I			N		S			D		F		M
A		U		E	T	C	E	T	E	R	A	
L	E	A	R	N		R		E		R		N
	A		B		H	A	M	P	E	R	E	D
G	R	O	A	N		C		S		A		I
	L		N		T		E		R		N
A	S	P	E	C	T	S		A	X	I	N	G

5

S	U	B	T	L	E	T	Y		A	X	E	D
	P	R		M		E	S		S		V	
A	G	O	U	T	I		A	N	S	W	E	R
	R		C		N	O	R		A		N	
H	A	C	K	E		E		S	Q	U	A	S	H
	D			N				L			
F	E	R	R	E	T		L	A	T	E	S	T
			E			U				I	
L	O	G	J	A	M		L		S	I	Z	E
	R		O		E	E	L		T		Z	
L	I	A	I	S	E		A	F	I	E	L	D
	B		N		T		B		L		E	
Z	I	P	S		S	P	Y	G	L	A	S	S

2

S		S		V			C		B		O
C	R	E	D	I	T		C	O	L	O	U	R
R		C		N		P		N		O		D
A	N	O	D	Y	N	E		T	A	B	L	E
T		N		L		R		E		Y		R
C	O	D	E		B	E	A	N	O			S
H		S		C		G		T		C		S
			C	H	A	R	M		F	O	O	T
U		T		O		I		S		R		A
S	C	R	A	P		N	A	T	U	R	A	L
E		I		P		E		A		E		L
R	O	C	K	E	T		O	R	A	C	L	E
S		K		R			R		T		T	D

6

	R	E	J	O	I	N	D	E	R	
S		L		P		E		M		D
T	E	M	P	E	R	A	T	U	R	E
A			N		R		L		P
N	E	T	T	L	E		F	A	I	R
D		R		Y		D		T		E
A	X	E	D		R	E	N	E	W	S
R		A		T		A				S
D	E	S	T	R	U	C	T	I	V	E
S		O		I		O		R		D
	U	N	B	O	U	N	D	E	D	

3

D	U	M	P	L	I	N	G		E	A	T	S
	P		L		N		R		N		E	
O	S	I	E	R	S		O	R	G	A	N	S
	C		A		H	O	W		I		E	
F	A	C	T		O		N	I	N	E	T	Y
	L				R		E					
R	E	V	I	S	E		A	B	S	U	R	D
		N		Q		U		A				
I	G	U	A	N	A		J	A	P	E	
	E		N		B	A	A		I		T
S	C	H	E	M	A		R	E	F	L	U	X
	K		L		S		I		F		R
D	O	Z	Y		H	E	A	V	Y	S	E	T

7

M	A	L	I		A		E			I		A		D
	N		N	O	N	F	L	A	M	M	A	B	L	E
K	N	I	T		O		M		P		E			F
I			E		D	I	S	C	R	E	E	T	L	Y
S	H	O	R	T	E	N		A		T		I		
	I		W			T		S		U	N	I	F	Y
D	A	T	A		R		I			W	I	S	H
	T		V	E	R	D	I	G	R	I	S		E
S	I	R	E	N		I		A		P		N
	O			E		C		T	E	N	A	N	T	S
A	N	T	I	M	A	T	T	E	R		P		E
N		O		I		I		R		E	R	N	E
E	N	T	R	E	P	R	E	N	E	U	R		C
W		S		S		R		D		S	E	E	M

4

I	S	L	A	N	D		S	C	A	M	P	I
M		E		E		N		A		I		M
P	L	A	C	E	B	O		P	D		A
O		R		D		N	E	T	T	I	N	G
S	I	N	G	S		S		U				E
E		I		N		E		R	O	L	E	S
		N		P	I	Q	U	E		I		
C	I	G	A	R		U			S		P
O			E		I		E	N	T	E	R
H	A	B	I	T	A	T		A		E	E
O		Y		E		U	R	G	E	N	C	Y
R		T		N		R		E		E		E
T	R	E	N	D	S		G	R	A	D	E	D

8

F		G		I			D		B		A
I	C	I	C	L	E		F	I	L	L	E	D
E		M		I		M		L		A		D
L	A	M	B	A	D	A		E	D	D	I	E
D		I		D		C		M		E		D
E	A	C	H		G	A	M	M	A		
D		K		C		D		A		E		A
			A	H	E	A	D		C	L	A	M
A		G		E		M		F		E		A
L	I	L	A	C		I	L	L	E	G	A	L
G		E		K		A		A		I		G
A	M	B	L	E	D		C	I	C	A	D	A
E		E		D			L		C		M

9

T	U	C	K
R			E
A			Y
P	I	G	S

10

C			W
U	R	G	E
L			S
M	U	T	T
I			C
N	I	R	O
A			U
T	E	E	N
I			T
O	M	A	R
N			Y

11

```
B   B   C       B   G   B
A B O A R D   B Y P L A Y
S   N   I   L   A   E   T
S T U B B L E   N O B L E
O   S   S   T   D   E   S
O B E Y   S T A B S
N   S   T   E   Y   B   B
    B E A R D   B O R E
C   I   N   B   A   U   N
L I B R A   O B L I Q U E
U   S   B   X   I   U   A
B E E T L E   O B J E C T
S   N   E       I   T   H
```

12

```
E   I   B       E   C   P
M I S H A P   E X U L T S
B   O   N   C   P   I   A
A L L E G R O   A W F U L
R   A   S   N   N   F   M
K I T H   A S I D E
S   E   P   T   S   J   H
      V O C A L   H A L O
G   U   S   N   F   G   S
U P S E T   C R O Q U E T
T   I   M   Y   X   A   E
S Y N T A X   Z E B R A S
Y   G   N       D   S   S
```

13

```
B   G   S       R   L   B
E U R O P E   D E D U C E
E   E   I   S   C   N   V
S H A C K L E   I R A T E
W   T   Y   R   T   R   L
A X E D   G I V E N
X   R   S   O   S   A   L
    B O N U S   A D Z E
E   L   U   S   L   J   A
Q U I F F   L A Y O U T S
U   S   F   Y   R   D   H
I M P E L S   W I G G L E
P   S   E       C   E   D
```

14

```
  C H O C K A B L O C K
D   O   L   S   E   A   A
I   T   E A S E D   P A R
M E D I A   I   G   R   R
I   O   R   S   E L I Z A
N E G L E C T S       N
I   S   D   R   C   G
S       E S T I M A T E
H I G H S   T   V   R   M
I   A   A   A   I M B U E
N I B   U N T I E   I   N
G   L   N   O   R   D   T
  R E P A T R I A T E D
```

15

```
  L   R   G   Q   O   K
M I S U S E   U N L O A D
  M   B   L   I   D   R
J E E R   I   Z E B R A
  I   W   O   O   O
  C H A I N   Y A K S
  V   I   A       E
D E M I   F I V E S
  N   G   E   N
  T R U T H   E S P Y
  U   A   O   A   E   I
B R O N C O   X E R X E S
  E   A   F   E   S   R
```

16

```
B   A   A       C   C   B
A T T A C K   B E S I D E
N   T   R   C   R   D   S
A M E R I C A   A D E L E
N   M   D   T   M   R   T
A L P S   B A S I S
S   T   C   M   C   C   B
    B Y W A Y   C O V E
B   C   N   R   A   P   E
A L I B I   A F F L I C T
T   G   C   N   I   O   L
C R A V A T   A R O U S E
H   R   L       E   S   S
```

17

	C	A	R	A	P	A	C	E	
	L		C		S		G		
T	I	G	H	T		S	T	R	I	P
R		A		S		A		E		E
E	W	E	R		K	I	L	T	E	R
L			S		L				I
L	A	Y	M	A	N		S	K	E	W
I		E		F		M		N		I
S	A	M	B	A		A	L	O	N	G
		E		R		L		T	
		N	O	I	S	I	E	S	T	

21

S			D
Y	E	T	I
N			S
D	I	S	C
I			U
C	O	W	S
A			S
T	A	X	I
I			O
O	P	E	N
N			S

18

A	K	I	M	B	O	V	E	R
I	S	E	S	T	A	T	E	S
L	I	T	E	D	E	A	L	C
A	D	T	R	A	S	N	Y	R
E	E	X	T	O	I	S	O	A
R	R	E	N	O	L	M	U	W
E	A	I	H	T	O	O	N	L
N	N	S	R	E	T	S	G	A
G	I	S	K	S	I	R	E	Y

19

D	I	L	L
I	D	E	A
L	E	V	Y
L	A	Y	S

22

I	N	C	H		S	P	E	C	I	F	I	C
N		H		C		L		A		A		H
D	R	A	C	H	M	A		A	C	C	R	A
E		I		A		I		I		T		R
S	C	R	A	M		C	O	R	P	O	R	A
C			P		E		V		R		C
R	E	C	O	I	L		C	O	R	S	E	T
I		O		O		D		Y			E
B	A	L	A	N	C	E		A	C	T	O	R
A		O		S		C		N		U		L
B	U	N	C	H		I	N	C	E	N	S	E
L		E		I		D		E		I		S
E	C	L	I	P	S	E	S		A	C	E	S

23

E	N	J	O	Y	S		C		K		E
X		E			P	L	A	N	N	I	N	G
H	O	T		I		D		O		E
O		S	N	E	E	Z	E		C	U	R	B
R		A		S		N		K		G
T	E	M	P	O		A	C	R	O	N	Y	M
		L		P		E		U
T	I	T	A	N	I	C		S	T	A	V	E
	G		T		A		A		L		A
Q	U	A	Y		Z	O	D	I	A	C		R
A		P		Z		I			O	F	F
I	N	C	U	B	A	T	E		V		U
A		S		S		U	N	W	E	L	L

20

K	I	N	G
E			A
R			U
B	O	W	L

24

P	O	N	C	H	O		P		M		E
U		I			F	A	L	L	I	B	L	E
R	A	P		T		E		S		E
S		P	I	G	E	O	N		M	O	V	E
E		E		N		A		A		E
S	E	D	G	E		W	R	I	T	I	N	G
		L		Z		Y		C
S	C	R	A	P	E	D		C	H	E	E	K
	R		C		S		G		J		L
M	A	L	I		T	O	R	Q	U	E		A
Y		A		F		A			C	O	X
C	O	N	T	O	U	R	S		T		O
N		E		L		P	E	R	S	O	N

25

```
M U S I C   W E L L O F F
E   E   O   H   O   I
L   V   N E   Q U A R T
B R E A T H E S   D   E
O   N   E Z   T E N S E
U N T E S T E D   R   V
R   H   T     R O E
N     L   E N C U M B E R
E I D E R   E   B L   Y
  N   G   R E A B S O R B
A C T E D   S   I   N   O
  U   N     O   N   G   D
T R O D D E N   G U S T Y
```

26

```
B R I L L I A N T
A     A   I   E     E
B I P E D   R E L I C
Y   O   Y   B   E   O
S W I M   M A R G I N
I   S   M   G   R   O
T R O W E L   P A L M
T   N   T   L   P   I
E P O C H   A S H E S
R   U   O   G       T
  S I D E S H O W S
```

27

```
A C A C I A   M   B   C
C   F     H E A D A C H E
I L L   E   G   L   A
D   A L K A L I   L A C E
I   M   D   C G   H
C H E E K   G A L A H A D
    L   G   L   M
C E D I L L A   L E M M A
  L   G   A   F   E   G
M I D I   C A L M E D   L
  J   B   I   A   I C E
C A L L B A C K     A   A
  H   E   L   E M B L E M
```

28

```
T O Y S
O P E N
Y E T I
S N I P
```

29

```
M O W S
O P A L
W A R E
S L E W
```

30

```
W A I F
O     E
R     L
M U S T
```

31

```
C       C
R A V E
I       R
M A G E
I       M
N E R O
O       N
L O K I
O       O
G U R U
Y       S
```

32

```
D R A M A S   A D O R E D
E   D   I   I   E   E   I
T R O D D E N   S D   E
A   P   E   D O C T O R S
C I T E D   U   E     E
H   I   S   N A D A L
    O   D A T E D   O
D I N G O   R     W   G
O   L   I   D I N A R
T O R P E D O   O   T   A
I   U   F   U N W O U N D
N   D   U   S   E   R   E
G A D F L Y   G L A N D S
```

Solutions

33

A	V	O	I	D	S		P	A	S	S	E	D
G				E		A		J				E
H		S	T	E	A	D	F	A	S	T		L
A		U		P		A		R		E		U
S	U	B	M	E	R	G	E		F	L	U	X
T		T		N		E		Q		E		E
	O	R	D	E	R		Q	U	I	P	S	
K		A		D		R		A		H		T
N	I	C	K		B	A	R	I	T	O	N	E
I		T		H		Z		N		N		A
G		S	E	A	W	O	R	T	H	Y		S
H				U		R		E				E
T	H	R	I	L	L		G	R	I	N	D	S

34

N	O	B	O	D	Y		Z	E	B	R	A	S
Y				O		L		X				T
M		R	E	M	A	I	N	I	N	G		I
P		U		I		F		T		R		N
H	U	M	A	N	I	T	Y		F	A	N	G
S		I		A		S		T		C		Y
	K	N	I	T	S		C	R	E	E	P	
A		A		E		J		U		L		T
S	E	N	T		F	O	R	S	W	E	A	R
I		T		A		I		T		S		I
D		S	E	V	E	N	T	I	E	S		P
E				O		T		N				L
S	Q	U	A	W	K		I	G	N	I	T	E

35

S	I	E	R	R	A		L		R		A	
A		L			P	R	E	T	E	N	D	S
L	E	A			H		A		A		M	
V		P	L	A	I	N	S		S	A	I	L
E		S			D		H		S		R	
R	E	E	D	S		R	E	F	U	G	E	S
			O		U		D		R			
A	C	C	O	U	N	T		S	E	P	I	A
	L		R		C		G			I		D
T	O	P	S		L	Y	R	I	C	S		R
	S		T		O		U			T	W	O
D	E	S	O	L	A	T	E			O		I
	T		P		K		L	I	N	N	E	T

36

S	T	A	R	S	A	N	D	S	T	R	I	P	E	S
A		U		L		I		I		E		E		T
V	A	R	N	I	S	H	E	D		P	O	S	E	R
I		I		P		I		I		R		E		A
N	A	C	H	O		L	E	N	I	E	N	T	L	Y
G		L		F		I		G		S		A		E
S	W	E	E	T	E	S	T		T	E	A	S	E	D
				H		M		E		N				
S	Y	S	T	E	M		K	N	I	T	T	E	R	S
P		U		T		C		F		A		P		T
I	M	B	R	O	G	L	I	O		T	R	I	E	R
N		S		N		E		R		I		G		I
O	W	I	N	G		R	E	C	O	V	E	R	E	D
F		S		U		I		E		E		A		E
F	A	T	H	E	R	C	H	R	I	S	T	M	A	S

37

D		D		D				E		D		F
E	V	A	D	E	D		E	X	H	A	L	E
P		M		C		D		P		R		I
E	X	P	I	A	T	E		E	A	T	E	N
N		I		Y		P		C		S		T
D	E	N	Y		F	O	R	T	S			
S		G		E		S		S		D		E
			E	D	D	I	E		F	E	R	N
E		E		U		T		E		S		T
D	O	R	I	C		E	L	L	I	P	S	E
I		N		A		D		L		A		N
F	E	I	S	T	Y		D	E	P	I	C	T
Y		F		F				N		R		F

38

M	E	D	D	L	E	S	O	M	E	
O				A		A		O		
D	U	R	U	M		P	A	N	D	A
E		E		B		S		O		S
M	E	L	O	D	Y		U	T	A	H
		I		A		S		R		
P	I	G	S		R	E	P	E	A	T
I		I		G		A		M		O
E	R	O	D	E		S	H	E	E	N
		N		A		O				I
	A	S	T	R	O	N	O	M	I	C

39

I	M	P	U	D	E	N	T	I
S	N	A	C	K	A	R	M	G
U	G	H	Y	E	O	M	A	H
O	N	I	E	C	E	A	L	T
R	I	N	I	R	M	N	T	H
E	D	O	S	T	I	U	I	U
N	E	I	T	I	R	T	M	R
E	N	I	E	R	E	T	E	S
G	N	I	L	L	E	Y	A	D

40

C	U	T	S
U	R	S	A
T	S	A	R
S	A	R	I

41

```
M A I D
U _ _ O
S _ _ Z
H Y P E
```

42

```
R . C
E V I L
S . I
P R O M
O . A
N E S T
S . O
I D O L
B . O
L O N G
E . Y
```

43

```
. N . C . I . R . L . I
R E N O W N . O C E A N S
. V . N . G . G . V . S
D E F T . R O U L E T T E
. . . E . E . E . L . A
W A R M E S T . S C E N T
. M . P . S . C . R . C
B E L L Y . W A G O N E R
. R . A . P . P . S
O I N T M E N T . S A V E
. C . I . E . I . I . I
M A R V E L . V E N I C E
. N . E . S . E . G . E
```

44

```
S U B T L E . Y E A S T S
E . R . O . D . L . K . H
Q U O R A T E . I . I . E
U . C . M . M A X I M A L
I T C H Y . O . I . . V
N . O . . L . R I D G E
. . L . J O I N S . A
Z A I R E . T . T . R
E . . S . I . P L A C E
R I S O T T O . A . B . N
O . A . I . N I T R A T E
E . F . N . S . H . S . W
S L E I G H . U S H E R S
```

45

```
B E S E T S . W H I T E R
Y . N . A . E . O . U . A
P H O E N I X . R . T . I
A . O . K . T O R Q U E S
S I Z E S . R . I . . E
S . I . . A . F A W N S
. N . A P P L Y . R
U R G E D . O . . O . V
N . . H . L . B A N J O
C H I M E R A . R . G . I
L . S . R . T R A F F I C
O . L . E . E . I . U . E
G R E A S Y . A D D L E D
```

46

```
T H R E N O D Y . B E A M
. E . G . P . I . U . N
P A R R O T . E F F I G Y
. D . E . I L L . F . L
O M I T . M . D E A D E N
. A . . A . . L
U N F U R L . D R O O P Y
. . . S . . E . . R
A T T U N E . C . V I O L
. R . A . A L I . I . T
H A M L E T . D U T I E S
. W . L . E . E . A . I
P L O Y . R E D O L E N T
```

47

```
D I S A V O W A L
E . . . I . I . I . P
F L A K E . L E M M A
I . D . W . D . E . R
N A V Y . P L A S M A
I . I . P . Y . T . C
T U S S L E . J O S H
E . A . A . T . N . U
L O B B Y . E R E C T
Y . L . E . R . . E
. E N D A N G E R S
```

48

```
I M B I B E . M . D I D
I . I . A D E L E . E
C L I M B E D . A . C . C
. E . L . D . D E L H I
F A L L I B L E . A . M
. G . C . E . B . I . A
M E D I A L . M A M M A L
E . E . L . C . L . . C
D . C . C A L L B A C K
I L I A D . B . G . L
C . D . E . A M A L G A M
A . E M A I L . M . I
L E D . L . B E C A M E
```

49

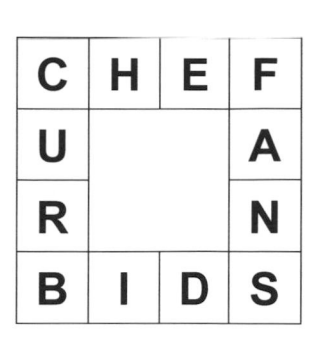

```
C H E F
U     A
R     N
B I D S
```

50

```
A     C
B O N O
O     N
M E A D
I     I
N E S T
A     I
T R I O
I     N
O R C A
N     L
```

51

```
T A C K
A G U E
C U R L
K E L P
```

52

```
S E A T
E D G E
A G E S
T E S T
```

53

```
G   S   A     F   A   F
R A T I F Y   C O N F E R
A   A   T   C   R   F   A
T A F F E T A   E D I F Y
I   F   R   R   S   X   S
F L E D   F E A T S
Y   D   F   F   S   A   G
      F O C U S   A F A R
A   F   R   L   A   F   A
F L I N T   L I F T O F F
I   L   I   Y   O   R   T
R E L I E F   F O N D L E
F   S   S       T   S   D
```

54

```
  I N H A B I T A N C Y
S   E   P   N   X   R   C
H   S   P E D A L   A A H
O U T E R   O   E   Z   E
W   I   I   O   S T Y L E
M I N I S T R Y       R
A   G   E       J   B   L
N       E S C A P A D E
S I F T S   Q   Y   S   S
H   L   O   U   W A S P S
I V Y   C H I N A   O   L
P   E   K   R   L   O   Y
  D R E S S M A K I N G
```

55

```
O P E N E D     Z   H O W
  L   M   A R E N A   A
F A W N I N G   R   R   Y
  T   G   R   O X B O W   A
D E F O R M E D   O   U   R
  A   A   E   V   U   R
T U N I N G   J A R R E D
U   E   T   S   N   N
E   G   C L I Q U I S H
S O L V E   I   U   I
D   E   L   T R I L O G Y
A   C A K E S   S   N
Y E T   S   T H E I S T
```

56

```
G L O W W O R M   A G U E
L   R   O   O   A   A
U R B A N   N U Z Z L E S
E   I   D   D   L   T
    T   T E   O U T S I D E
D E S I R E S   A   C   R
I   I   N   X   L
S   B   N   T R O L L E Y
P L O U G H S   N   A
R   R   E   O   Z   C
O V E R A C T   M O U T H
V   R   S   I   L   E
E L S E   K E R C H I E F
```

57

```
R E C O M M E N D A T I O N
O   U   E N   E R   N     T
L A R G E S T   T R A M C A R
L   R   K   R   H   N   E   E
I R I S   D E P R E S S I O N
N   C   T   E   O   C   N   D
G A U G E D   E N T R E A T Y
    L   L   I   E   I   B
A Q U I L I N E   S P I L L S
G   M   I   N   B   T   U   I
A D V E N T U R E R   S E E N
S   I   G   E   L   S   M   C
S I T D O W N   I M P L O D E
I   A   F   D   E   U   O   R
  S E L F C O N F I D E N C E
```

61

```
D       E
I D O L
S       A
C R A B
R       O
E W E R
P       A
A U N T
N       I
C I A O
Y       N
```

58

```
G R U N G E   H I D I N G
A     A   I   S       R
U   I N T E N D I N G   U
C   M   H   S   S   R   M
H A P P E N E D   G A S P
O   E   R   T   H   V   Y
  G L U E S   H A B I T
H   L   D   G   R   T   H
I B I S   G R A D U A T E
R   N   H   E   C   T   L
I   G U A C A M O L E   I
N       T   T   P       U
G A L O S H   G Y P S U M
```

62

```
G U Z Z L E     G   F O G
  P   O   G U A N O     R
A G I T A T E   F   R   I
  R   T   N   F L A G S
L A U G H T E R     G   T
  D   I   S   A   E   L
S E W I N G   S L U D G E
T   A   G   G   L   L
A   S     M A G E L L A N
G A T E S   M   R   N
I   I   A   U R G E N C Y
N   N I G H T   E   E
G I G   E   I N G E S T
```

59

```
A Q U A M A R I N E
Z     E   U   I
T E P I D   E I G H T
E   A   A   D   H   U
C O L D L Y   S T A G
    A   S   T   C
M I T E   F R O L I C
A   A   S   A   U   H
R O B O T   D U B A I
    L   A   E       M
  M E M B E R S H I P
```

63

```
R W A N D A   O   I V Y
  A   I   B O X E R   E
C R U I S E R   E   I A
  F   P   A   N A D I R
F A N D A N G O   T U E
  R   T   S   T   U   E
S E L E C T   R H Y M E D
Q   O   H   J   R   Q
U   G     V E N O M O U S
A M B E R   A   T   E
S   O   A   N E T W O R K
H   O O Z E S   L   R
Y A K   E   D E L A Y S
```

60

```
F A C T S
R       P
O       I
W       K
N U D G E
```

64

```
T I M I D   S O J O U R N
O   I   A   P   G   O
O   S   I R   W R A T H
L I F E S P A N   E   O
B   I   I   N   U S U R P
O U T W E I G H   S   O
X   S   S     A   D   L
E   V   U B I Q U I T Y
S N E A K   R   U   V E
  O   L   R E F E R E E S
S T O V E   E   O   R T
  C   E   Z   U   S   E
G H A S T L Y   S M E A R
```

65

```
D E P O T S . . F . O A T
. L . A . T I L T S . R
V I S I B L E . A . M . A
. T . L . N . N O O K S
D I S P E N S E . S . H
. S . T . E M . I . E
S T A T O R . . S E N S E D
W . N . P . T . T . N
A . N . . B R E A T H E S
L A U R A . I . P . M
L . A . X . B A H R A I N
O . L O O S E . O . E
W A S . N . . D R O W S Y
```

66

```
C A T T L E . A S S O R T E D
E . O . E . . I . V . E . A
N O R M A L . A S S E S S O R
O . P . K . . T . R . T . T
T R E S S E S . E N D G A M E
A . D . . U . R . R . T . D
P R O C R A S T I N A T E
H . . A . C . N . W . . A
. M I S C E L L A N E O U S
P . I . P . P . A . . R . T
H A L I B U T . W A Y S I D E
O . I . E . . I . E . F . R
B A T H R O B E . P A N I N I
I . I . R . . L . S . C . S
A N A L Y S E S . S T R E A K
```

67

```
B . M . M . . D . L . B
A C A C I A . B E C A M E
G . C . M . B . C . B . L
G L A C I A L . I D E A L
A . D . C . A . B . L . E
G L A D . A C H E D
E . M . G . K . L . H . C
. . G A M M A . E A C H
L . C . M . A . F . G . I
A D L I B . I L L E G A L
D . I . L . L . I . L . L
L A C K E D . A C C E D E
E . K . D . . K . D . D
```

68

```
O B D U R A C Y E A R
R B S T R A D D L E B
U S S E R E C A P D O
B E R E A M E R R O O
U R T I S E E E I L K
S D S M L S R M S C S
E N R O E E I O O E U
I A E N O C E V N X R
N H T S I G E R E P V
E E G A T S E D O L E
D E V E I R P E R O Y
```

69

```
H O G S
O H I O
G I R L
S O L E
```

70

```
W A F T
A C R E
F R E E
T E E N
```

71

```
T A G S
A C N E
G N A W
S E W S
```

72

```
T R U M P
H . . . L
I . . . A
C . . . Y
K N O W S
```

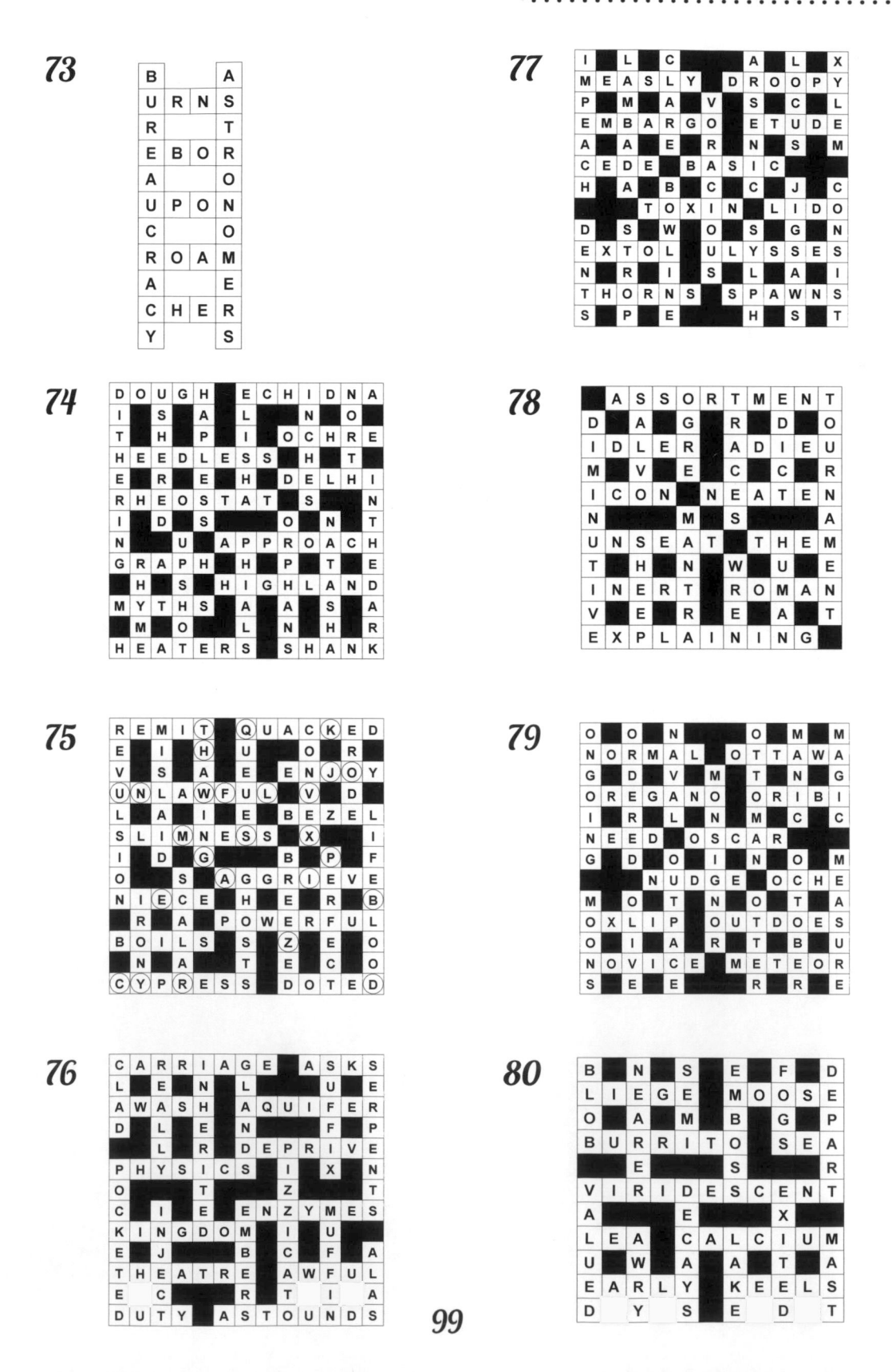

73

	B			A	
U	R	N	S	
R			T	
E	B	O	R	
A			O	
U	P	O	N	
C			O	
R	O	A	M	
A			E	
C	H	E	R	
Y			S	

77

I		L		C			A	L		X
M	E	A	S	L	Y		D	R	O	O	P	Y
P		M	A	V	S		S	C		L
E	M	B	A	R	G	O		E	T	U	D	E
A		A		E	R	N		S		M
C	E	D	E		B	A	S	I	C	
H		A	B	C		C		J		C
			T	O	X	I	N		L	I	D	O
D		S	W		O	S		G		N
E	X	T	O	L		U	L	Y	S	S	E	S
N		R		I	S		L		A		I
T	H	O	R	N	S		S	P	A	W	N	S
S		P		E			H		S		T

74

D	O	U	G	H		E	C	H	I	D	N	A
I		S	A	L		N		N		O
T		H	P	I		O	C	H	R	E
H	E	E	D	L	E	S	S		H		T
E		R		E		H		D	E	L	H	I
R	H	E	O	S	T	A	T		S		N
I		D	S		O		N		T
N		U		A	P	P	R	O	A	C	H
G	R	A	P	H		P		T		E
	H	S		H	I	G	H	L	A	N	D
M	Y	T	H	S		A		A		S		A
M		O		L		N		H		R
H	E	A	T	E	R	S		S	H	A	N	K

75

R	E	M	I	T		Q	U	A	C	K	E	D
E		I		H	U		O		R
V		S	A	E		E	N	J	O	Y
U	N	L	A	W	F	U	L		V		D
L		A		I		E		B	E	Z	E	L
S	L	I	M	N	E	S	S		X		I
I		D		G		B		P		F
O		S		A	G	G	R	I	E	V	E
N	I	E	C	E		H		E		R		B
	R		A		P	O	W	E	R	F	U	L
B	O	I	L	S		S		Z		E		O
	N		A		T		E		C		O
C	Y	P	R	E	S	S		D	O	T	E	D

76

C	A	R	R	I	A	G	E		A	S	K	S
L		E		N		L		U		E
A	W	A	S	H		A	Q	U	I	F	E	R
D		L		E	N		F		P
		L	R		D	E	P	R	I	V	E
P	H	Y	S	I	C	S		I		X		N
O			T			Z		N		T
C		I		E	E	N	Z	Y	M	E	S
K	I	N	G	D	O	M		I		U
E		J		B			C		F		A
T	H	E	A	T	R	E		A	W	F	U	L
E		C			R		T		I		A
D	U	T	Y		A	S	T	O	U	N	D	S

78

	A	S	S	O	R	T	M	E	N	T
D		A		G		R		D		O
I	D	L	E	R		A	D	I	E	U
M		V		E		C		C		R
I	C	O	N		N	E	A	T	E	N
N			N		M		S			A
U	N	S	E	A	T		T	H	E	M
T		H		N		W		U		E
I	N	E	R	T		R	O	M	A	N
V		R		E		E		A		T
E	X	P	L	A	I	N	I	N	G	

79

O		O		N			O		M		M
N	O	R	M	A	L		O	T	T	A	W	A
G		D	V		M		T		N		G
O	R	E	G	A	N	O		O	R	I	B	I
I		R		L	N		M		C		C
N	E	E	D		O	S	C	A	R	
G		D	O		I		N		O		M
			N	U	D	G	E		O	C	H	E
M		O		T		N		O		T		A
O	X	L	I	P		O	U	T	D	O	E	S
O		I		A		R		T		B		U
N	O	V	I	C	E		M	E	T	E	O	R
S		E		E			R		R		E

80

B		N		S		E		F		D
L	I	E	G	E		M	O	O	S	E
O		A		M		B		G		P
B	U	R	R	I	T	O		S	E	A
			E			S			R
V	I	R	I	D	E	S	C	E	N	T
A			E			X
L	E	A		C	A	L	C	I	U	M
U		W		A		A		T		A
E	A	R	L	Y		K	E	E	L	S
D		Y		S		E		D		T

81

```
T I G E R
H       A
U       N
M       K
B L O W S
```

82

```
B       C
R U S H
O       O
N A I L
Z       E
E A R S
M       T
E L L E
D       R
A L T O
L       L
```

83

```
L U N C H I N G   K I E V
I   I   A   O     M     A
R E M I T   T O P S P I N
E   B   C   I     U     I
    L   H   O B L I G E S
G R E M L I N   O   N   H
L   I       U           E
I   F   N   C H I P P E D
T R I G G E R   S   A   M
T   D       I   I   N
E N G I N E S   A L I B I
R   E       I   N   N   N
Y E T I   E S C A P I N G
```

84

```
B O N F I R E S     J A D E
U   A   N   V     L     Y
M I M I C   O X I D I S E
P   E   U   L     G     B
    L   M   V O U C H E R
P A Y A B L E   N   T   O
E       E     Z     W
R   E N   Q U I C H E S
J U J I T S U   P   I
U   E         A P K   I
R A C C O O N   I D E A S
E   T       T   N   R   L
R I S K   L A R G E S S E
```

85

```
  P   C   P   U   I   C
S A L A M I   M I N N O W
  P   R   M   B   T   N
G A R B   P E R C E I V E
      O   L   A   R   E
U P E N D E D   F J O R D
    E   I   S   M   E   G
G R A F T   Q U A C K E D
    O   E   S   S   T
E X E R C I S E   I N C H
    I   O   Z   U   O   H
A D D U C E   M O N D A Y
    E   S   D   S   S   T
```

86

```
U M P I R E S   K A Y A K
T   O   A     I   O   I
T O T E M   S L A C K E N
E   E   P   T   N   E   G
R A N D   O R E   U S E D
        C   I   E   A   O
C   Y A C H T S M A N   M
O   O   Y   C   Y   A
N U L L   S H E   S T O P
T   I   O   E   D   A   A
E M P O W E R   R I S K Y
N   I   L     A   H   E
D O D O S   C O M P A R E
```

87

```
        I       S   D
E N N U I   P O T T E R Y
M   S   N   R   I   B   O
A B D I C A T I O N   O P U S
R   D   P   M   G   N   T
R O D E N T   E P I T A P H
I       M   N   I
L I G H T F I N G E R E D
    O   R   N       E
A P R I O R I   A K I M B O
W   M   P   S   D   O   A
B A L L   I N T I M I D A T E
R   E   C   E   I   I   E
D E S P A I R   T E N O R
S       L       E
```

88

```
  A   A D   A   F   C
A L I C I A   C H A C H A
  G   I   M   M   C   A
L A I D       E M A I L
  I   D       D   I
    C L I M B   E A C H
F   A   A   E       E
H I G H   L L A M A
E   A       M   C
L E M M A       A C H E
  A       I   F   C
F E L L E D   E L I J A H
  D   L   E   D   A   L
```

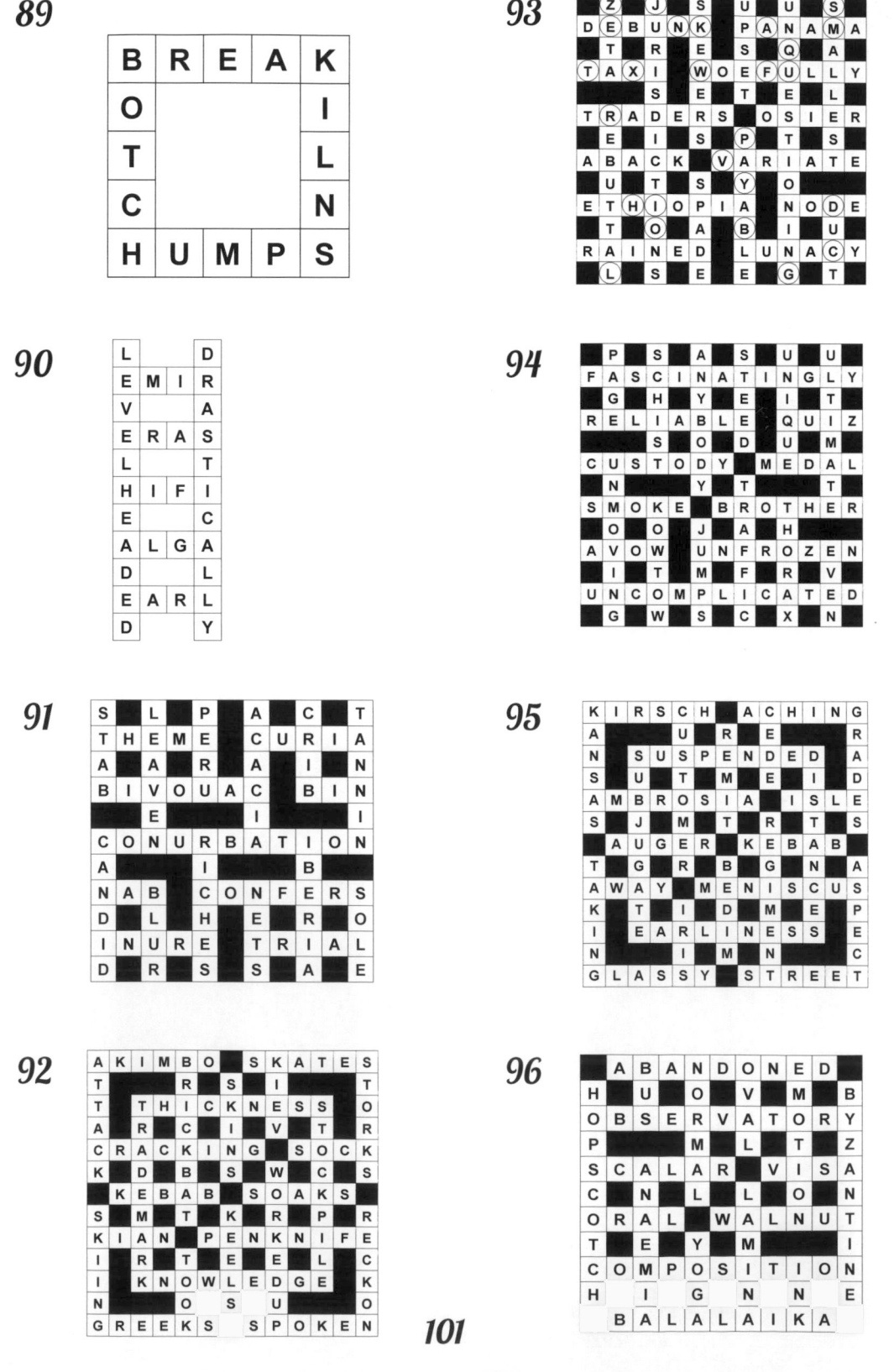

89

BREAK
O · · · I
T · · · L
C · · · N
HUMPS

90

L · · D
EMIR · R
V · · A
ERAS · ·
L · · T
HIFI · ·
E · · C
ALGA · ·
D · · L
EARL · ·
D · · Y

91

S · L · P · A · C · T
THEME · CURIA
A · A · R · A · I · N
BIVOUAC · BIN
· · E · I · · I
CONURBATION
A · I · · B ·
NAB · CONFERS
D · L · H · E · R · O
INURE · TRIAL
D · R · S · S · A · E

92

AKIMBO · SKATES
T · R · S · I · T
T · THICKNESS · O
A · R · C · I · V · R
CRACKING · SOCK
K · D · B · S · W · S
· KEBAB · SOAKS
S · M · T · K · R · R
KIAN · PENKNIFE
I · R · T · E · E · C
I · KNOWLEDGE · K
N · · O · S · U · O
GREEKS · SPOKEN

93

Z · J · S · U · U · S
DEBUNK · PANAMA
· T · R · E · S · Q · A
TAXI · WOEFULLY
· S · E · T · E · L
TRADERS · OSIER
· E · I · S · P · T · S
ABACK · VARIATE
· U · T · S · Y · O
ETHIOPIA · NODE
· T · O · A · B · I · U
RAINED · LUNACY
· L · S · E · E · G · T

94

P · S · A · S · U · U
FASCINATINGLY
· G · H · Y · E · I · T
RELIABLE · QUIZ
· · S · O · D · U · M
CUSTODY · MEDAL
· N · Y · T · T · T
SMOKE · BROTHER
· O · O · J · A · H
AVOW · UNFROZEN
· I · T · M · F · R · V
UNCOMPLICATED
· G · W · S · C · X · N

95

KIRSCH · ACHING
A · U · R · E · R
N · SUSPENDED · A
S · U · T · M · E · D
AMBROSIA · ISLE
S · J · M · T · R · T · S
· AUGER · KEBAB
T · G · R · B · G · N · A
AWAY · MENISCUS
K · T · I · D · M · E · P
I · EARLINESS · E
N · I · M · N · C
GLASSY · STREET

96

ABANDONED
H · U · O · V · M · B
OBSERVATORY
P · M · L · T · Z
SCALAR · VISA
C · N · L · L · O · N
ORAL · WALNUT
T · E · Y · M · I
COMPOSITION
H · I · G · N · N · E
BALALAIKA

97

S	I	R	E	S		T	E	S	T	A	T	E
U		E		A		O		R		I		
B		S		I		U		S	U	R	L	Y
S	H	E	R	L	O	C	K		N		E	
C		R		O		A		S	K	I	R	T
R	E	V	E	R	E	N	T		S		E	
I		E		S		T		R		E		E
P		S		S	T	U	R	G	E	O	N	
T	R	I	P	S		E		I		C		A
	I		A		S	N	A	P	P	I	N	G
S	N	O	R	E		N		L		T		E
	S		S		I		E		A		R
S	E	L	E	C	T	S		T	O	L	L	S

98

D	E	B	U	G
A				L
M				I
P				N
S	H	O	R	T

99

P			E
H	O	A	X
O			C
T	A	M	E
O			E
G	L	A	D
R			I
A	X	O	N
P			G
H	A	I	L
Y			Y

100

H	A	I	L
A	I	R	Y
I	R	O	N
L	Y	N	X